Pathways to Leadership

Pathways to Leadership

A Leader's Journey to Success

Louis J. Pepe

ROWMAN & LITTLEFIELD
Lanham • Boulder • New York • London

Published by Rowman & Littlefield
An imprint of The Rowman & Littlefield Publishing Group, Inc.
4501 Forbes Boulevard, Suite 200, Lanham, Maryland 20706
www.rowman.com

86-90 Paul Street, London EC2A 4NE, United Kingdom

British Library Cataloguing in Publication Information Available

Library of Congress Cataloging-in-Publication Data

Title: Pathways to leadership : a leader's journey to success / Louis J. Pepe.
Description: Lanham : Rowman & Littlefield, [2022] |
    Includes bibliographical references. | Summary: "Pathways to Leadership
    delivers strong advice, valuable guidance, and successful strategies
    to equip any leader to become better at leading teams and managing
    organizations"—Provided by publisher.
Identifiers: LCCN 2021045537 (print) | LCCN 2021045538 (ebook) |
    ISBN 9781475854336 (cloth ; alk. paper) | ISBN 9781475854343
    (paperback ; alk. paper) | ISBN 9781475854350 (epub)
Subjects: LCSH: Leadership.
Classification: LCC HD57.7 .P454 2022 (print) | LCC HD57.7 (ebook) |
    DDC 658.4/092—dc23
LC record available at https://lccn.loc.gov/2021045537
LC ebook record available at https://lccn.loc.gov/2021045538

This book is dedicated to my grandchildren,
Carter, Kaila, Eloise, and those to come.

"Congratulations! Today is your day.
You're off to Great Places! You're off and away!"
– Dr. Seuss, Oh, the Places You'll Go!

In life, we do not always know the road before us or where our journeys will
bring us based on the decisions we make—but trust that the better prepared
we are, the more enjoyable the trip and more rewarding the destination.

Contents

Foreword

I have discovered in my many years in leadership development that people frequently make two fundamental errors. First, some use the terms "leadership" and "management" interchangeably. That is incorrect, though a Venn Diagram does exist between the two. "Management" is focused on work standards, resource allocation, and organizational design. It is about controlling complex institutions and often the use of data to make decisions and choices.

"Leadership" is about vision, motivation, and trust. Its focus is on change and moving both people as well as organizations into the future. Consequently, effective leaders must constantly seek to balance the immediate needs of their organization with an eye on how they are preparing their team to meet the challenges of the future. That is particularly important at this moment of historic change.

The second error is to talk about "leadership training" as opposed to "development." Training is the action of teaching a person a particular skill or, possibly, a type of behavior. That is accomplished through repetitive effort until the "student" achieves a level of proficiency or expertise.

Pathways to Leadership makes neither error. It underscores the critical fact that leadership development is a lifelong effort. It is a journey without a final destination, and the book's primary focus on the leader developing him or herself makes this an invaluable contribution to the study of leadership.

As we embark on the leadership journey, it is common to ask a critical question—what skills make a great leader? This book will help any leader wrestle with this age-old question. There are also many lists of leadership competencies, but two stand out. General Norman Schwarzkopf, commander of all US and Allied forces during the Gulf War, returned to his alma mater, West Point, in 1991 and addressed the Corps of Cadets. He told those future leaders that two competencies were fundamental—character and competence. The pages of *Pathways to Leadership* further develop the general's wise counsel.

This journey requires leading yourself and defining at the onset what you wish to accomplish individually and collectively as a leader. The external challenges of leadership in a rapidly changing environment are enormous, but the biggest problem may be internal. How does the 21st-century leader achieve harmony between the competing demands of his or her position, family, and personal well-being?

Effective leaders realize that they must do this to ensure they bring the "best of themselves" to their team and not the "rest of themselves"! Doing so also sets an important standard for the team and gives everyone "permission" to do so as well.

In conclusion, I have had the pleasure of knowing Lou Pepe for over a decade and enjoyed our frequent conversations about leadership development. Lou brings his passion for leadership as well as his over thirty years of experience as a manager, team builder, and strategist to this task. As a result, this book is a conceptual as well as pragmatic approach to effective leadership, and the capstone to Lou's Reality-Based Leadership effort. You will find it enriching. Enjoy this wonderful journey!

Jeffrey D. McCausland, PhD
Founder and CEO, Diamond6 Leadership and Strategy, LLC
Author, *Battle Tested! Gettysburg Leadership Lessons for 21st Century Leaders*

Preface

What is the requisite time necessary to plan and chart a course for advancement in the pursuit of becoming a leader? Is it measured in weeks, months, or years? Is it dependent upon knowledge, strength, connections, or determination? I find it is a combination of all of the above. While it is never too late to become a leader—or if already a leader, becoming better—leadership takes time, focus, attention, and giving of yourself to others.

Concerning time—anything worthwhile takes time, and some are faster studies than others. Sure, skill, drive, and initiative find rewards quicker in a world thirsty for leaders who excel at achieving goals and objectives in any organization; however, to lead, you must first prove you can follow. Second, you need to convince others that you are up for the task, that you have acquired the skills necessary to lead others, and possess the common sense to know what is worth pursuing and what is not.

Otto normal verbraucher is an old German expression meaning "the average person," used to convey the sentiment of a "reality check" when a normal person wouldn't consider it, because it doesn't make sense or lacks common sense. That is the wisdom of leadership and that is what we look to in this book, *Preparing to Lead.*

The Bible speaks of a *treasure of common sense* available to the honest who are shielded by walking with integrity (Proverbs 2, verse 7); in life, pathfinders, trailblazers, and voyagers are all leaders at different stages of a journey with varying degrees of skill, experience, knowledge, and wisdom. How these leaders apply common sense throughout their professional life will dictate how high they will rise and to what degree they can avoid setbacks.

Failure is not falling, but refusing to get back up (Chinese proverb). Falling is a part of learning to walk, and walking is a part of learning to run. Getting up and trying again will allow us to move forward. Common sense.

As pathfinders we determine how to get where we want to go and begin to acquire the foundational skills necessary to head out on our own as we blaze trails, along with the experiences and knowledge acquired to make our journeys successful.

As trailblazers we pioneer new ideas, advise those who rely on us for our counsel and advice, and show the way to others.

As voyagers we chart new journeys to new discoveries and go where others won't—into the unknown and beyond.

REALITY BASED LEADERSHIP (RBL)©
A CONCEPTUAL FRAMEWORK OF COMMON SENSE!

The RBL series is written based on my 30 years of management experience in building, managing, and leading teams to achieve desired outcomes while completing tasks, implementing strategies, and accomplishing goals. This is necessary in any organization to accomplish the ultimate objective—the mission.

Each book is meant to provide a glimpse into differing facets of organizational management that allows for continued success through refinement of skills promoting operational awareness in today's rapidly evolving world of business.

Embarking on leadership is to set out on a path that takes time, patience, and endurance. Wanting something is not enough; you must fight for it and rise up from each defeat only to grow stronger in your resolve and dedication to achieve what you believe is possible, despite what others try to convince you is not.

It is not an easy journey, but one filled with trials including baptism by fire at times and uncertainty from situations that prepare us to do better over time and become the type of leader that knows what others do not; knows how to find it; and how to apply it, to the right degree at the right time. Though the path is long, hard, and lonely at times, it is one worth pursuing, and gives rewards found nowhere else. It is less traveled and, trust me, more difficult; however, as Robert Frost wrote, "That has made all the difference."

Acknowledgments

Special thanks to my editors: Tom Koerner, senior editor; Carlie Wall, managing editor; and my proofreader, Jeannine Dotten.

Thanks to the people who helped me most when I needed it: God; my wife, Jean Johnson; Oscar Lewis, aka OL; Joe Gerbaraux; and David G. M. Clover.

Introduction

Leadership remains an important function of management. Today more than ever, we need leaders who understand the culture, climate, and change in today's challenging world.

Pathways to Leadership delivers strong advice, valuable guidance, and successful strategies to equip any leader to become better at leading teams and managing organizations. The resources found in this book are geared toward new as well as seasoned leaders. Individuals looking for ways to become more adept at developing the skills necessary to lead, survive, and thrive within companies and organizations will benefit from this book.

Anyone intent on learning how to be an effective and successful leader will enjoy moving through this journey. From pathfinding to trailblazing, to learning not only why we need to take breaks and recharge, but how to accomplish this while maintaining high levels of productivity.

Given the unprecedented challenges facing business leaders in all industries, leaders need to find and hold on to balance while remaining focused, responsible, and accountable for the success of their organizations. As a result, leaders need to find purpose, develop critical skills, and apply knowledge in ways that move teams forward and keep organizations relevant.

This book is the fifth and last book in the series of Reality-Based Leadership (RBL)© books written to share strategies and proven techniques for managers and leaders at all levels within any field of business.

The concepts, principles, and ideas shared are rooted in years of experience, and the knowledge gained serves as a foundation for success across a wide range of applications.

PART I

Pathfinders

Chapter 1

Life, Knowing What You Want (and Finding the Path to Take You There)

Pathways allow us to get where we need to go by delivering us to predetermined places in our travels and in our lives. Some paths become famous routes that ensure getting us from point A to point B without fail. Some less-traveled ways provide excitement and wonder, yet still offer a degree of protection from the dangers that exist because someone else has blazed the trail by taking the first steps, leaving a path for us and others to follow—we call these people leaders.

Other pathways exist to take us where we want to go to reach new heights, gain new experiences, and deliver us to a place that gives us fulfillment.

I know a place. *I'll Take You There* was released in February 1972 by a group named The Staple Singers, and it promised a path to a place where there "ain't nobody cryin' and ain't nobody worried." While the song was written by Stax Records vice -president Al Bell following the funeral of his little brother who was shot to death—it became an anthem for everyone that wanted to find a place to escape the troubles of the times, or find love and happiness as portrayed in the film, *Children of a Lesser God*. Its power was to transport our mood by uplifting our spirit and therefore moving us, even if temporarily to a better place.

Today certain pathways are recognized as critical routes to success, progress, and happiness such as education, certification programs, research, relationships, and family, to name a few.

Milton Bradley capitalized on this thought in the 19th century, creating one of the most popular board games still played today, the Game of Life, created in 1860.[1] It would get a makeover in 1960s and become the game we all know today with the two-track immediate decision of going to work for the "quick buck" or taking the longer path to acquire a "career" and receive a bigger "payday."

The premise is quite simple; it is all about following certain paths to become a millionaire and live out your days at "Millionaire Acres" or risk it all on attempting to become a "Millionaire Tycoon" and instantly win the game on a spin of the wheel or simply end up on the "Poor Farm."

Chock-full of moral guidance, the game delivers both positive and negative reinforcement of messages about education, work, risk, and reward, all centered on achieving money and therefore happiness. While money does not guarantee happiness, it is important to acquire enough to pay the bills, reach our goals, and secure our future.

In its simplest terms, the game made an impact on many of us growing up and left me in particular with the notion that education and family equated to a better standard of living that puts us on the path to happiness, thus avoiding the poor farm.

More importantly, it demonstrated the need to follow certain pathways to acquire your goals, and that nothing comes easy and there are certainly setbacks; however, if you stay the course and work to achieve the desired outcomes it works. The same can be said for becoming a leader.

You don't just wake up one day and decide to be a leader—-you must prepare for it and you must be ready to take on the responsibility for others that comes with it. It takes strong dedication, discipline, study, and practical experience to develop a certain set of skills. Then you need to hone those skills, and master them to succeed.

Realizing this is the first step to finding your path to leadership, acquiring the ability to lead in today's challenging environment is the second.

Know where you're going. . . have a plan and stick to it! Pathways to leadership predominantly involve entry and mid-level leaders; however, executives looking to change career paths can also benefit from the information in this book. It is written to equip readers interested in pursuing leadership opportunities with practical guidance and a commonsense approach to leadership. Designed to be that "go-to reference" for building and maintaining a rewarding career, it is focused on smarter approaches to challenges and practical advice to better navigate landmines.

Acquiring the opportunity to become a great leader involves scouting opportunities that are all around us. Leadership programs today are plentiful and offer the type of opportunities that can help you determine if leadership is right for you and, if so, how to gain skills necessary to lead others. So what are some of these pathways? How do we access them? And most importantly—where can we find them?

COMMON PATHWAYS TO LEADERSHIP

1. Workplace Opportunities—Taking advantage of opportunities in the workplace is a quick and easy way to get noticed by taking on more responsibility, and demonstrating your ability to handle leadership roles. "An employee who is always looking to lead while also performing well at her job could be on a fast track to greater opportunities. Employees showing drive and determination often end up as managers or move into other roles offering greater respect, responsibility and pay. Employees focused on career growth should make achieving leadership opportunities a primary objective."[2]

   Many in-house opportunities are available through committee work or volunteering to spearhead a particular exercise or present on a topic at a department training. Some opportunities are as simple as demonstrating leadership in preparing and executing tasks that go beyond your job description, yet are helpful to your boss and beneficial to the company or organization.
2. Workshops on Leadership—Talk to your supervisor about signing up for professional development workshops or conferences where PD opportunities include leadership training.

   A willingness to go demonstrates initiative and desire for self improvement; however, in some cases persuading your boss to approve your attendance can be a real challenge. Many organizers recognize this and provide helpful hints to assist potential registrants to build their case for attendance.

   Show your supervisor exactly how attending the workshop or conference will yield a positive return on investment for your group, company, and/or organization. Need help finding a reference point to start drafting the request? Start by reviewing the brochure or workshop description and presenting the request in writing along with information focusing on what you intend to learn, how you will bring that knowledge back and apply it in your office, department, or organization.

   This not only documents your efforts to improve your performance by learning leadership skills, it represents ROI for the group or company. If this continues to be a problem—consider going to another company that appreciates your desire to learn, grow and move up.
3. Professional Organizations and Associations—Professional groups provide excellent opportunities for members to gain access to leadership round tables, panel discussions, break-out sessions or general sessions. Many individuals believe they must be a member to participate and that is not always true. However, the costs are

typically higher and borne by the individual, absent company sponsor-
ship, but well worth gaining leadership exposure and knowledge.

    If already a member of these groups, get active and participate by
learning, sharing, and networking as you acquire skills that can be
applied in a leadership role in the future or one now if you are new to
leadership.

4. Online   Leadership   Courses—These   pathways   are   easily found in an online search with various offerings ranging
from leadership institutes to higher education institutions.

    Here are just three top-rated online courses reported by Balance
Careers, an online informative group that is part of the Dotdash[3] digital
media company that publish articles and videos about various subjects
across categories:

- Coursera—Coursera Strategic Leadership and Management
  Specialization, chosen by Balance Careers[4] based on affordabil-
  ity, are university-based leadership courses without pre-requisite
  requirements and application for new managers who need in-depth
  training. "Its top-rated leadership class, Strategic Leadership and
  Management Specialization, is designed for those new to supervision
  and management."[5]
- The Center for Creative Leadership (CCL) is Balance Careers' Best
  Overall Choice based on "Top-tier leadership development courses in
  all formats—live, onsite, blended learning—and across all leadership
  dimensions, from basic supervisory and management skills to team
  leadership."[6]
- Udemy—Selected by the group based on the extensive selection of
  leadership courses and world-wide availability, along with the fact
  that courses are taught by industry experts. What they liked about
  Udemy is summed up in three points: affordable courses taught by
  industry experts, number of courses that provide a certificate of
  completion, and course attendee ratings.

Other available online course programs include: Class Central, FutureLearn,
LinkedIn Learning, The American Management Association (AMA),
TrainUp, and many more, proving anyone interested in exploring any of these
pathways are just a click away from beginning their journey.

With respect to a seasoned leader in one industry looking to change course
and advance down a new path towards a second career, the following story
has become a familiar one over the years with individuals who know where
they want to go, but are not sure how to get there.

This is an example of a success story that started with an individual who
was determined and open to suggestion, pointers, and advice. He remained

persistent in networking to aid in his quest. An established executive in the communications/broadcast industry, he wished to change careers. He became a school board member in his community and developed an interest in school district operations and more specifically a desire to become a school business administrator.

Being one of many colleagues in the field that he reached out to, our conversation centered on his experiences, transferable skills and his desire to make the change. Having enough time behind him (experience) and more than enough left in the tank for a second career (longevity), the transition was not only possible but made sense. The conversation took us into what kind of experience(s) he had that prepared him for what was to come and what elements of the job-related experiences he lacked that would need to be remedied through professional development (PD), certification courses, and mentoring.

While the details, rules, regulations, and requirements of the job require study—the ability to manage people, in this case, high achievers—is a critical skill that must be inherent. That same skill set is a pre-requisite for providing guidance, direction, and recommendations to those same individuals.

As we spoke further, I realized many of the attributes he possessed were those that would serve him or anyone well in the position he sought: in particular, his ability to work with board members, other administrators, staff, and the public based on his prior experiences.

The outcome was success as his quest ended six months later when he was appointed in high-performing K–12 school district as the assistant school business administrator. It worked—persistence paid off!

Exposure provides the magic of discovery by ensuring we know what's out there and, as a result, what we wish to pursue. The takeaway for this gentleman is the same for any of us interested in pursing new paths regardless of where we are in our career or where we have been. Logic dictates that unless we know about something's existence, we will never have the ability to decide whether we are interested in pursing it.

The roads we have traveled do not have to be considered separate and apart from where we are going—they can be connected through those experiences. A road is never a dead end. There is always a path that will allow you to redirect your drive and start you off on a new journey.

Chapter 2

Certified, Bona Fide, and Recognized

Why Certs Matter

In order to move along our chosen pathways and take on higher-degree challenges, steeper paths, or more difficult ones, we need to acquire knowledge, tools, and equipment. At the same time our experiences, defeats, and victories along the way allow us to acquire the skills necessary to navigate, overcome obstacles, and ultimately succeed in our endeavors.

The Legend of Zelda comes to mind. Not only was it one of the most popular games Nintendo ever produced, it epitomized the stages of discovery through journey by acquiring key objects or items that were essential to survival and moving onward through new and more challenging pathways.

As we search for pathways to head out on our journey in life for a career that fulfills us and meets our needs, we need the same degree of preparation we put into trips. Like any trip we go on we need to pack, and not just anything—we look for the things we need, the things we cannot do without, what we call the essentials.

We start by consciously considering an inventory of what we have on hand, where it is stored, and what we may need to go out and get. This goes hand in hand with what store(s) to go to, based on the availability of products, location, and lead time, as some items require pre-order to ensure their availability for our trip.

By ensuring we have what we need when we need it, we head out on our journey with confidence, excitement, and high expectations for success, joy, and fulfillment. While we look forward to pleasure trips, the same degree of planning and packing goes into business trips for the same reason.

Consider getting to the hotel the night before a big meeting or interview and realizing you forgot your belt, shirt, or blouse or worse yet . . . your shoes. Running down to the gift shop can take care of toiletries or aspirin albeit you'll pay a premium; but forgetting essentials like clothing can become a nightmare or at the very least a scavenger hunt that ends in either a major investment by paying a steep price or a marathon trip to multiple stores that are hopefully open and have what you need in stock. Either way it adds stress to the trip and has the potential to put a dark cloud over the entire outing.

As we plan our careers and look to advance, we need the same degree of planning, attention to detail, and focus to ensure our journeys are successful and each trip becomes meaningful. This requires picking up certifications that matter along the way.

Certifications provide the legitimacy we need to secure the jobs we want—they serve as official documents attesting to a status or level of achievement that we have obtained. For most select job opportunities they are required or preferred, and when we have them, they allow us access to restricted paths that those without them cannot enter.

Preparing to lead is all about making oneself ready for what lies ahead by equipping oneself with the essentials of leadership. This takes time and, like anything worthwhile, it requires thought and preparation to acquire the necessities to lead successfully.

Certifications are a definite on the "list of essentials" since they go to the heart of one's authority to lead. They become credentials that provide immediacy in accepting someone's qualifications, achievements, and qualities. Although they are associated primarily with resumes, they are equally important to those we supervise as they represent validation in our ability to lead and give us license to lead them as we become "bona fide" versus being considered "inexperienced" or "green."

They provide backup and support in answering the typical questions associated with any new leader: *"Who are you to be in charge?" "Why should we follow you?" "What experience do you have?" "Are you equipped to lead us?"*

These questions can be muttered in dissatisfaction by detractors or kept silent by others who are simply waiting to pass judgment as they size up any new leader.

Great leaders recognize this fact and work to overcome it by gaining the trust, confidence, and a willingness from others to follow them based on their abilities displayed over time as their teams successfully overcome major challenges—but it takes time.

Certifications can help shorten that time and help gain that trust, because they (certifications) are easily recognized and accepted—depending on the nature and importance placed on the certificate. Initials after your name on letterhead, signature blocks on an email, or business cards signify experience and mastery of a particular skill set.

In order to have value they must have meaning and connection to the association, field, or trade of those possessing them. A certificate in forestry is worthless to an auditing firm, much like a CPA will likely not help you get a job as a forest ranger.

Collecting certifications that have no meaning in your field of employment are worthless unless they are in a field you wish to transfer into.

When it comes to obtaining certifications, time is money and some are not cheap—so plan accordingly and do a little research prior to jumping in to collect certifications to paper your wall. Go after the ones that are recognized, in demand, and carry weight in the industry or field you are currently in or the one you wish to transition into.

A certification can be just -the -ticket for entry to a given field that allows one to combine their skill set with credentials in a way that produces trust, confidence, and "street cred."

Today professional certifications are a part of almost every industry. The International Society for Automation, for instance reports, "Certification recognizes and documents your experience, knowledge, and education—-and provides an objective, third-party assessment of your skills."[1]

Indeed.com, the number 1 job search engine according to Career Sidekick,[2] founded by Executive Recruiter Biron Clark, informs users that business certifications are "Industry-recognized credentials" that can be used to demonstrate "abilities in different areas" thus allowing individuals to "stand out in the crowd." Or, as another top search company, ZipRecruiter puts it, "The needle in the haystack."[3]

While the importance of obtaining certifications is growing, each field has specific designations that have become easily recognized and synonymous with quality and assurance that employers are looking for. In the tech field for instance, a Certified Solutions Architect—Professional or (AWS) could be the ticket for a wide array of jobs through Amazon or any other giant in the tech field. It ranks at the top of the list for CIO's Top 15 IT certifications in demand for 2021.[4]

In April 2013 Amazon launched the first AWS Certification Program with the first of several exams that it made available that year. Eight years later Google is joining in with its launch of a professional certification program allowing people to earn the equivalent of a four-year degree in six months.[5] Both West Coast tech giants continue to trade in the thousands of dollars per share, indicating a healthy outlook as they grab more and more market share and now expanding into the teaching world. With Google trading at slightly over $2,000 a share[6] as of March 2021, and Amazon at over $3,000 per share[7] for most of the past year (2020), their combined entry into the world of certifications promises their relevance will only increase in the decades ahead.

From 1950 to 2008 the percentage of the workforce holding a professional certification climbed from 5% to 25%.[8] Today they are more in demand than ever with more than 43 million people in the U.S. alone holding a profession certification or license in 2018, according to the U.S. Bureau of Labor Statistics (see figure 2.1). "The prevalence of occupational licenses, common in fields such as healthcare, law, and education, has risen substantially over the past 50 years."[9]

Keep in mind that certifications, like anything worthwhile, can be held to the *rule of acquisition*—the harder they are to come by, the more value we place on them. Advanced degrees or professional certifications that involve seat-time, academic rigor, and testing require time and investment that typically results in higher compensation. Anything obtained too easily or certifications that lack gravitas reduce the impact or effect, and they must be backed by a reputable group or institution and be industry-recognized to become a "door opener" or an "escalator."

Other factors to consider in our quest for certifications is "shelf-life," as certain industries such as technology continue to evolve at break-neck speed, rendering some certifications useless in a matter of a couple years.

Labor force participation rates of people 25 years and older, by professional certification and licensing status and educational attainment, 2018

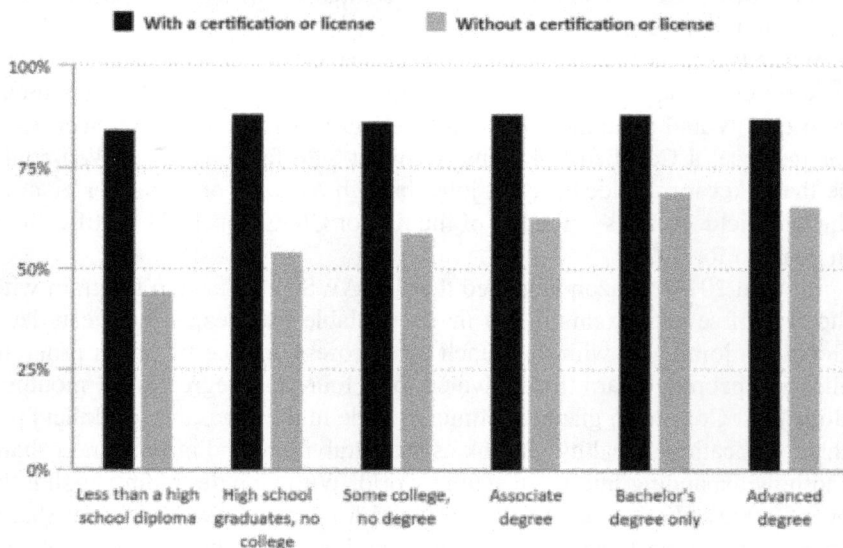

Figure 2.1. Labor force participation rates by certification and licensing status and educational attainment, 2018 annual averages. *Source: U.S. Bureau of Labor Statistics.*

In an 2015 online career advice article that appeared on Dice.com, a leading website for technology careers, the point was made by the author that "The evolution of technology makes many certificates obsolete pretty quickly" (with some exceptions—some software, like the Linux kernel, doesn't change all that rapidly).[10]

A clear takeaway from the article is that you need to consider the Return on Investment (ROI) before plunging in with time and money. So you need to do some homework and research the certificates that will add value and *open doors* as you move through various stages of your career.

So where do we go to get the certifications that matter? And how do we advance in our quest to gain credentials necessary to compete and succeed beyond established degrees from higher educational institutions?

Begin with an understanding of the power of "micro-degrees" or "micro-masters"—these are credentials that are career specific and are comprised of one or more sources of accelerated educational experiences. They are great ways to save both time and money in supplementing an earned degree to enhance your value and increase your attractiveness to recruiters.

Another source of meaningful pathways lies with professional associations and can be easily found on their websites under the professional development tab.

MasterClassManagement.com is another source that is becoming attractive as a free online option for business management training and leadership skills courses that offer certificates under the "Master Certificate" designation taught by industry experts in the field. With a self-paced style of learning, you get the benefit of proceeding according to your schedule.

Now that we covered the where, lets focus on the how to:

First, start by taking an inventory of your profession by searching out the certifications that are in demand. Most professional associations list certifications and classes or course work governed and approved by the association for the credentials that matter within the particular industry.

The Association for Financial Professionals, for example, administers the FP&A cert. or "Financial Planning & Analysis" certification.[11] As their website states it is "The only credential for FP&A practitioners, created by FP&A practitioners." Their call -to -action is simple yet effective: "Validate your unique skillset with the FPAC credential."[12]

In the case above, the certification can be a "door opener" if one is new to the industry and trying to break in or can be used as an "escalator" allowing upward mobility within the industry for an experienced member to gain access to jobs with larger organizations.

Second, research opportunities for continuing education by pursing accredited online courses such as MOOC (Massive Open Online Courses). Mooc.org is an extension of edX.org, a leader in online courses, and best of all they are FREE! With more than 2,900 courses to choose from they provide an affordable and flexible way to learn new skills, advance your career, and deliver quality educational experiences at scale.[13] Of course, if you are looking for a certification, they charge a modest fee—so there goes the free.

With the backing of highly accredited learning institutions like the Massachusetts Institute of Technology, Harvard, Berkeley, Brown, Georgetown, Dartmouth, and Princeton, to name a few, and topics ranging from Business Administration to Blockchain, and from Cloud Computing to Structural Engineering, there is a course that allows individuals to build their skills and move them forward, upward, and onward.

So if you have an eye on career development and are looking for a fast escalator or simply looking to change careers and need a quick door opener—these courses can be a game changer in providing the "X" factor in moving your resume to the *top of the pile*.

In a January 8, 2021, article appearing on CIO.com as "Today's Top Story—Top 15 IT certifications in demand for 2021," the author states, "Whether you're just starting out and building your resume or you've been in the industry for 20 years, there's a certification that can help boost your salary and your career."[14]

Leading the list of the most highly sought after certs are: AWS Certified Solutions Architect—Professional, Certified Cloud Security Professional (CCSP), and Certified Data Privacy Solutions Engineer (CDPSE).

Certifications, while hot in the IT industry, are finding just as much allure and importance in other industries as we move toward a climate of certified professionals in the 21st century.

In the same week, Business.com reported out on the Top 8 Certifications for business, claiming, "A business certification can make your skills stand out and help you get the right salary."[15] The list includes:

1. Certified Associate in Project Management (CAPM)
2. Certified Business Analysis Professional (CBAP)
3. Certified Supply Chain Professional (CSCP)
4. Project Management Professional (PMP)
5. SAP Certified Application Associate—Business Planning and Consolidation
6. Salesforce Certified Administrator
7. HubSpot Inbound Marketing
8. Oracle Certified Professional (OCP)

Today certifications are becoming a *must-have* for attainment and advancement in almost every industry for a reason: Certifications help the advancement of the industry by increasing prestige, value, and compensation for the professionals associated with that industry.

At the same time, certifications are becoming an increasing factor in the selection criteria that allows employers another measure of skill, performance, and motivation for prospective hires as well as in-house candidates as they demonstrate gained competencies and signify commitment to the profession.

The team at Glassdoor weighed in with a July 2020 post stating their consensus: "Certifications certainly *can* make a difference, but not all certifications are created equal,"[16] reporting from interviews with top recruiters that "Some certifications can actually move the needle in their decision to hire a candidate—if one of them is relevant to your field, consider looking into it!"[17] Great advice!

Chapter 3

What Makes a Leader Great?

Skills Required to Lead

Great leaders possess a unique skill set to move organizations forward by rallying the troops to achieve extraordinary outcomes that average leaders can never obtain. It starts with a mission-oriented philosophy of putting the needs of the organization and those who serve it first. "Leaders have the unique ability to put others first and motivate a team to rally around a cause. While many aspire to leadership, not everyone can be a leader."[1]

Being a true leader requires self-sacrifice and the ability to motivate, guide, and lead others in the process to achieve what needs to be done—that requires a set of skills, determination, and desire to serve others in a way that adds value to our organizations and provides us with purpose and meaning.

Difficult tasks require great skill, expertise, and knowledge of the subject matter to produce a positive outcome and achieve the desired results. That is why we have specialists who are called in for difficult surgeries to assist, perform, or consult with challenging operations or treatment plans that extend beyond what is considered common or basic.

Great leaders need an arsenal of skills that require routine as well as occasional use depending on the task at hand or emerging crisis. While our goal as leaders is to avoid a crisis at all costs—the reality remains, they happen, and we must be prepared to deal with them when they do. How well we rise to the occasion and how well we respond to those crises is largely dependent upon our training, specific skills set that we have acquired, and our ability to apply those skills in a way that addresses those crises in a clear, concise, and effective manner.

When it comes to a skill set—you can't go out and buy it, you have to build it!

So what are these skills that every leader needs to acquire? Are they qualities or characteristics? They are a blend of both. A blended approach in acquiring and applying both the qualities associated with great leadership and characteristics found in great leaders provides the formula for success in leadership by giving leaders the foundation necessary to take on challenging roles.

So how do we become practiced in the manner expected of our positions as leaders? We become practiced by doing, succeeding, failing, understanding how to improve, and doing it again and again until we get it right, and then get better, faster, and more efficient at getting it done. Like the specialists in the above example, organizations rely on our ability and knowledge (skills) to assist with the overall mission of the organization.

Similar to the specialists assisting with consults, as successful leaders, our quality traits help to differentiate and separate us from our peers, thus making us more desirable to work with, depend on, and learn from.

As a leader, you need to reach that point to become truly valuable to the unit, company, or organization to truly be an effective leader.

Let's put a fresh perspective on leadership and what you need to get the job done. The Top 10 blend of skills and characteristics that work beyond learned behaviors to match up with practical application provides a basis for great leadership.

This blended list of skills and characteristics provides holistic leadership to deal with challenges that come our way as leaders, by providing essential talents that are crucial for key issues that arise within and outside of our organizations.

Let's start by examining the skills that continue to top any list of the "best of the best" or great leadership: Communication, Delegation, Integrity, Motivation, Team Building, Empathy, Flexibility, Innovation, Positivity, and Vision (see figure 3.1).

1. COMMUNICATION (Skill): in leadership, a "must skill" as it is a core concept, and without it we lack the ability to address the basics of *Who, What, When, Where, Why,* and *How.* Communication provides a *corridor for understanding* and it goes both ways. It allows us to convey *what* needs to be accomplished, *who* needs to do it, *how* it should or will be accomplished, *when* and *where* it needs to be accomplished, and most importantly—*why.*

   If we do not explain why we need things done, individuals do not receive the value of importance with respect to the vision and reason behind the work that needs to get done.

   A skilled leader knows how and when to interject each element of understanding to keep projects moving and teams on track for success.

   The corridor allows feedback to ensure we understand where others are on the path, the challenges they face, and how to improve situations to avoid a botched project or catastrophic loss. That requires effective

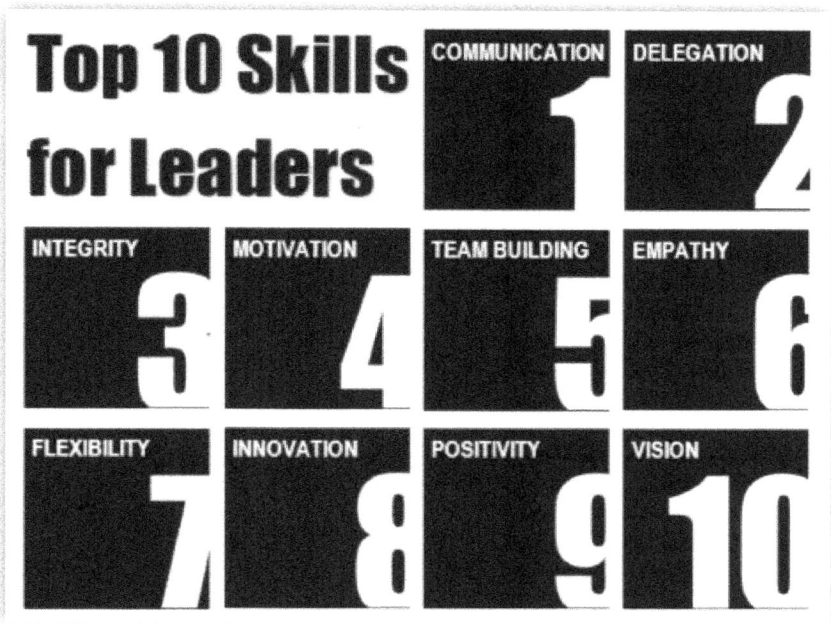

Top 10 Skills for Leaders

COMMUNICATION 1	DELEGATION 2
INTEGRITY 3	MOTIVATION 4	TEAM BUILDING 5	EMPATHY 6
FLEXIBILITY 7	INNOVATION 8	POSITIVITY 9	VISION 10

Figure 3.1. Top ten blended skills and characteristics needed for great leaders.

listening, and why I started with this premise in the first book of the series, *Avoiding Poor Decisions Through Effective Listening.*

2. DELEGATION (Skill): an important and essential skill that empowers our people and frees us up to manage more of the operation. This is perhaps the hardest skill to learn, and even harder for new leaders to apply as they tend to want to control every aspect of the jobs/projects they oversee.

Keep in mind the distinction between authority and responsibility— *you can delegate authority but never responsibility!*

The takeaway—As leaders we retain the responsibility for the overall success of our teams and the projects/work produced by those teams.

While delegation is essential to completing projects on time and within budget, follow-up is crucial to ensure the work that has been delegated is getting done, and done right.

When leaders fail to enforce this concept, it can cost them their job or even career. When we witness this up close it serves to remind us how imperative it is to career survival. We learn from these situations what not to do in order to avoid a similar fate.

That is precisely what happened with an esteemed colleague who from outward appearances had it all going on. That was obviously not the case, as would eventually be revealed from conversations with those closest to the reason for that person's demise.

In short, the individual was let go because they failed to follow up and ensure things were getting done that they had delegated to others.

What is striking with this situation in any organization is that many new leaders or established leaders who benefit from strong teams become exposed when moving up to more responsibility that reveals their flaws. Lack of follow-up is major flaw that is difficult to hide and more difficult to recover from.

3. INTEGRITY (Characteristic): while not a skill, integrity is central to who we are and the trust we build, that allows us to interact in a positive way with staff, colleagues, associates, customers, stakeholders, and anyone we come in contact with while conducting business.

We will take a deeper look into integrity in chapter 6 based on its singular importance in leadership.

4. MOTIVATION (Skill):   an art that requires charisma, energy, and trust—or does it?

When we think of the perfect leader, most of us envision that extrovert who runs through the office with an air of confidence and an attitude that gives off a sense of positivity, shouting out things like, "Come on team—we can do this!" Sometimes that style of leadership works—sometimes it does not.

It depends less on the type of leader you are and more about what each individual in your charge responds to.

Based on the research of Myers-Briggs[2] producing the Myer-Briggs Type Indicator® (MBTI®), there are many different types of leadership styles, sixteen to be exact, eight dealing with extroverts and eight dealing with introverts. All sixteen are proven leadership styles that offer pathways to success, yet each offers different characteristics that uniquely identify their leadership style and different ways of connecting with their teams.

So while some leaders may not be so outgoing, they too possess a deep sense of responsibility and a proven track record of demonstrated leadership based on consistent performance that also garners support, trust, and confidence.

Motivation is about engaging our teams and ensuring everyone is involved in the process of goal attainment. It serves to motivate others to accomplish the tasks necessary to achieve the overall mission.

According to a recent Gallup poll on employee engagement, "34% of U.S. employees were engaged, along with 16.5% who were actively

disengaged——-a ratio of two engaged workers for every actively disengaged one."[3]

The takeaway here is simply to get to know your people and find
out what motivates them, but start with a self-assessment to identify
deficiencies you must address to possess the needed qualities to lead and
display the characteristics that build trust.

5. TEAM BUILDING (Skill): Without teams, we are alone, and going it
   alone retards our growth, diminishes our impact, and prevents us from
   achieving large-scale success.

   Teaming is such an essential skill that it provided the concept for the
   fourth book in this series, *Building the Right Team: Maximizing Human
   Resources*. The development of teams remains a crucial part of leading,
   and a skill that every leader needs to apply.

   It starts with professional development for the improvement of existing team members, sorting out those who are not interested or incapable
   of meeting the standards established by the organization, followed by
   strengthening hiring practices to attract quality replacements.

   The importance of team-building can be found in articles, blogs,
   and books, recognizing the need for it and the benefit to culture, performance, and productivity that it brings.

   The Team Building Directory is an online resource for anyone interested in corporate team building, team development, and training. They
   point out, "Creativity and innovation are very important in the world
   of business and good team-building can help increase it even among
   employees who would not consider themselves creative."[4]

   The group recognizes what many top organizations understand—
   that is, "team-building exercises that encourage collaboration help to
   develop teamwork which is crucial for creativity to thrive."[5]

   When the practice of collaboration becomes an integral part of
   any organization's makeup, it improves communication, allows for
   thoughtful and challenging conversations that push all who participate
   to aspire to reach new heights, and achieves results that alone would be
   inconceivable.

6. EMPATHY (Skill): deals with understanding and caring about what others are feeling and how those feelings impact their ability to function
   at optimal levels.

   Some leaders struggle with this, as they have a hard time holding
   people accountable while they are dealing with personal issues and tend
   to overcompensate with too much empathy when, truth be told, they are
   not doing the team member or themselves any favors, since both remain
   accountable for performance.

But it is a key part of being a great leader and it requires balancing empathy with our responsibilities. The bottom -line is, we need to ensure we are capable of recognizing the need for compassion.

You know empathy is a key element of leadership when the Department of the Army's Field Manual on Leadership Development refers to it 20 times, to include framing their values: "ADRP 6–22 defines character as factors internal and central to a leader, which make up an individual's core and are the mindset and moral foundation behind actions and decisions. Leaders of character adhere to the Army Values, *display empathy* and the Warrior Ethos/Service Ethos, and practice good discipline."[6]

Empathy is a skill required of all leaders regardless of their line of work. Every organization needs people who are willing, ready, and able to carry out the mission every day, and when a person or group are dealing with personal issues, they need help and support to maintain focus or get the extended help and time to deal with their issues before returning to work.

When we care about and care for those we are responsible for, we not only improve employee engagement, we gain their trust and loyalty while building a stronger connection.

The Center for Creative Leadership, a global nonprofit centered on effective leadership, analyzed data from 6,731 managers in 38 countries regarding the importance of empathy in the workplace. They found that empathy in the workplace is positively related to job performance. "Managers who practice empathetic leadership toward direct reports are viewed as better performers in their job by their bosses. The findings were consistent across the sample: those managers who were rated as empathetic by subordinates were also rated as high performing by their own boss."[7]

Character is defined in the field manual as *internal and central to leadership,* breaking down the framework (FM 6–22, Table 6-1)[8] into three distinct categories: Developmental Need, Standard, and Strength, recognizing the need for developmental skills related to leaders who "exhibit resistance or limited perspective on the needs of others. Words and actions communicate lack of understanding or indifference. Unapproachable and disinterested in personally caring for soldiers."[9]

Translate that need into our organizations, and you will find the effect is the same and therefore the identified strength in successful outcomes for Army leaders, "Attentive to other's views and concerns," is global and applicable for leaders in any organization. The evidence supporting the global vision permeates from a sense of civic responsibility well beyond the confines of the military bases as it includes, "Taking personal action to improve the situation of . . . *civilians, family members, local community, and even that of potential adversaries.*"[10] That is strength, that is character!

That is ARMY strong, and it's backed with a call to action (CTA) requiring leaders to train, coach, and counsel when needed and role-model empathy for others.[11]

You need to strive for the same level of commitment in our own organizations with our leaders, and what we as leaders of and within those organizations need to model to be great leaders.

7. FLEXIBILITY (Skill): This igets better with practice and produces better outcomes each time we deploy it as it allows for thought, analysis, and adjustments. When you put these three elements of decision-making together, we become nimble and responsive to the environments we work within.

   Leaders cannot achieve this skill without understanding and applying the benefits of a growth mindset captured in book 3 of this series, *Problem Solving Today*, highlighting the work of Carol Dweck, *Mindset: The New Psychology of Success.*[12]

   Flexibility allows leaders to focus on what makes sense today—at the moment—compared to what was when the plans were made or the projections forecasted in the past, regardless of whether that was ten minutes ago or ten months ago. It requires the ability to adapt, modify, and improve—that's why the U.S. Marine's slogan, 'Improvise, Adapt, and Overcome' allows them to maneuver in the heat of battle or when encountering changes in conditions that could jeopardize their plan and, ultimately, their mission.

   Adaptive leadership is centered on flexibility, and that skill is essential for any leader to succeed in challenging environments. "Adaptive leadership means seeing change not as an obstacle, but as an opportunity to focus on being ready. To thrive as a leader requires the ability to adapt to these changes and adjust to the new conditions."[13]

   As a skill, flexibility is required in planning for any success. Without it, we become hard-lined, disassociated from the reality that circumstances and conditions continue to change and evolve, and disconnected from the information others are trying to relay to us. That does not mean we bend at every challenge to our decision-making. It means we remain pliable when necessary, rigid when called for to protect the process of achievement, and uncompromising when it comes to our values.

   In today's competitive environment of instant access to information, markets, and stakeholders, we need to be flexible while planning for the future with an eye on the present to avoid coming up short when striving to reach our goals.

8. INNOVATION (Skill): serves as a tool for improvement, longevity, and discovery. Innovation keeps companies relevant and allows for the growth they need to compete in markets without the hefty price tag associated with its predecessor, invention.

A recent blog appearing on the Northeastern University Graduates Program entitled *The Importance of Innovation in Business captured the reason behind the importance of innovation in business today that seized on the need for flexibility as well, proclaiming, "We've all heard the phrase 'adapt or die' and for businesses to achieve success in today's modern world, this is a universal truth. Take, for example, the massive expansion in technological advancements in the past decade; because of this extreme growth, businesses have been forced to adapt and expand more than ever before."*[14]

Innovation helps growth, maintains relevance, and allows for differentiation from competitors, and that leads to longevity in any field or line of business. In public education that means attracting and retaining students when school choice is becoming more mainstream with the continuous expansion of charter schools, choice schools, and academies, not to mention private and parochial schools.

"Innovation means using new technology and using new ways of thinking to add value to an existing idea or product and to make substantial changes in society."[15]

But it is not limited to technology alone. We need to look at all aspects of our business, organization, and operations to innovate and become better and stronger at what we do. So what does this really mean?

Innovation allows us to take a look at what already exists (what's in place) and modify or improve it to meet changing needs. This includes examining our equipment, our systems, and our practices. We need to look at ways to change those applications to meet today's needs that didn't exist at the time of their development.

Policy, for instance, is a natural for evolution based on changes in the law, circumstances, or societal pressures. We don't typically throw out the entire policy as it was written, but instead modify or add/delete sections to address those changes and strengthen the application of the policy.

Technology is, however, a great example since it has consumed all aspects of our daily life. Need a quick example? Here is one we all use every day—smart phones. Smart phones or handy phones as referred to by Germans, Austrians, and the Swiss, started as mobile phones in 1983 with the Motorola DynaTAC 8000X, a bit bulky that came with a hefty price tag of- \$4,000.[16] By 1992, a decade later, Nokia mass produced the cost-effective 1011 model retailing at \$300[17] for consumers with the digital display handsets that slipped into your pocket. With the passing of the next decade, Sony Ericsson released the dT68i that included an innovative add on, a clip-on camera in 2002, for approximately \$580.[18] That innovation paved the way for turning the handy phone into a camera as well. A year later the business world was wowed by a device called the BlackBerry. This all paved the way for the first iPhone, introduced in May 2007.

So in a little over two decades, the mobile phone for a few has become "smarter," more versatile, and affordable for everyone—thanks to innovation.

9. POSITIVITY (Characteristic): an essential skill that is key to leadership as it creates a strong desire among our teams to perform at their best. Positivity in leadership inspires confidence in those leading by those being led. "Positive leadership involves experiencing, modeling, and purposefully enhancing positive emotions."[19]

Positivity generates and gives off a *positive energy* that energizes teams and creates an atmosphere of continued possibilities,- regardless of the challenges. In the words of Zig Ziglar, "Positive thinking will let you do everything better than negative thinking will." So let's go positive!

Regardless of the issues we face, as leaders, we have a choice. We can be negative or go negative, as these issues appear to worsen or become more complicated; however, the fact is, they don't change, but our attitude and how we react to those issues have a big effect on our teams and those around us. When we choose to be positive or go positive and stay positive, we win because we bring our teams with us in a positive way: to tackle difficult issues, improve our strategies to combat those challenges, and create solutions to our problems. This all stems from a positive energy mindset that expresses a sentiment of "yes we can" versus a defeated attitude of "no we can't."

10. VISION (Skill): Vision rounds out our list for leadership musts, because without it—one is not a leader, just someone in charge.

People in leadership positions who lack vision are merely managers that keep tasks moving and ensure operation goals and objectives are being met. Where they fall short of great leadership is in the development, planning, and setting of those goals. Without vision, we cannot see the path in front of us that could lead to better outcomes—we lack imagination. It is vision that gives reality to our dreams, and leadership that turns those dreams into reality.

Vision provides the purpose, direction, and reason for leading others in the pursuit of goals and objectives. Great leaders know how to operationalize that vision through others in the organization, which makes it possible to achieve at all levels within the organization utilizing the above skills, starting with communication and delegation.

"A vision is a practical guide for creating plans, setting goals and objectives, making decisions, and coordinating and evaluating the work on any project, large or small. A vision helps keep organizations and groups focused and together, especially with complex projects and in stressful times."[20]

In summary, these blended skills prepare us for any path in leadership, as they provide a strong foundation by equipping us to deal with a host of challenges. Once we recognize their importance, we begin to work as leaders, to master them by turning them into habits. Through practice, they become ingrained in our DNA. These ten essential leadership skills prepare us to move forward, take on bigger challenges, leave the established path, and blaze new trails.

PART II

Trailblazers

Chapter 4

Leading with Purpose, Intensity, Confidence, and Knowledge

Rangers lead the way! Talk about a slogan that encapsulates the elements of leading needed to blaze a trail: Purpose, Intensity, Confidence, and Knowledge pushed the 2nd and 5th Ranger Battalions forward, creating a path for the 2nd Battalion, 16th Infantry Regiment, and the 1st Infantry Division on Omaha Beach in Normandy, France.[1] The story of the Rangers permeates an understanding of heroism in the face of adversity, horror, and intense fear. It provides a perfect illustration of trust that allowed others to get behind leaders as they led the way to spearhead the beach landing on D-Day, June 6, 1944, during Operation Overlord. Their actions and those of 156,000 troops were the largest invasions ever assembled before or since by Allied troops (by sea and air) on five beachheads in Normandy.[2]

While nothing compares with the dangers of war and the sacrifice made by those who gave their lives for the freedoms we share today, there are takeaways from their valor and lessons in leadership based on their ability to lead in the most challenging of circumstances.

Army Rangers are indicative of leaders who blaze a trail, allowing others safe passage to their objectives. The Rangers' primary mission is to engage in close combat and direct-fire battles.[3]

That is what great leaders do, and they do it selflessly, not for medals or recognition, but because they can. By doing so, it gives them purpose and allows them to matter. For them, it means reaching the top of Maslow's pyramid of needs, therefore attaining self-actualization, and that means personal success.

As leaders, we need to lead with the same degree of purpose, intensity, confidence, and knowledge to create new pathways for the success of our teams and organizations moving them forward and protecting them from harm. When competent or "squared-away" leaders clear a path for others in the organization they are leading, and when they exercise the elements of leading outlined in this chapter, they are leading in the same way Rangers do by looking out for the welfare of their teams to ensure attainment of goals and objectives in support of the mission for that organization. It all starts with purpose.

Purpose is why we exist in any organization. It is demonstrated by what we bring every day and why we bring it. That purpose belongs to the organization and the individuals who serve it. From the perspective of the organization, that purpose is outlined in a job description, and the expectations equate to the compensation package offered, or it should—that is business. As long as individuals perform well, they continue to be rewarded, or they leave—that is reality. Their decision to stay or go is predicated on their purpose, whatever that purpose may be: opportunity, money, benefits, or prestige. If any of these rewards fall off or become stagnant—they lose interest and go in search of those needs elsewhere.

The elements of this business transaction (time/value) defines what leaders look for in any career or job. It is why we get up every day and go into the fray to advance our lives by acquiring our needs. It is a purpose that drives us to accomplish our goals, that when aligned with the organization or companies we serve, makes us unstoppable as leaders.

A singular purpose is powerful in that it becomes intense, thus providing focus, direction, and fuel, to keep us moving forward—even in the face of adversity. Courage is what keeps great leaders from abandoning their course, regardless of the challenges they face, doubts public or private, ridicule, or overt attempts to force them to yield.

Knowledge is what allows them to succeed where others fail based on the reality that they know something in a way such that they can apply that knowledge for the betterment of society, allowing their organization or company to profit, gain market share or, in the case of humanity, achieve social benefits.

Throughout history, we have seen example after example of leaders who exhibited this degree of *purpose, intensity, confidence,* and *knowledge*: Lincoln's battle to preserve the Union; Gandhi's resistance to Great Britain's rule to free India; Einstein's relentless pursuit of discovery until his dying day; Churchill's steadfast determination to rally his people and avoid defeat by Hitler; and Mandela's struggle to end apartheid and advocate for human rights in South Africa.

These are just some of history's most notable examples for which these elements of leading strengthened their resolve as leaders to accomplish incredible feats. We can gain perspective, knowledge, confidence, and purpose from their achievements as well as the struggles they endured and overcame in the process. Think of all the great quotes that have been shared by these and other famous leaders, known for the significant trails they blazed so other may follow. Quotes continue to be a source of inspiration for leaders, and here are just a few that speak to *flexibility, accomplishment, desire* and *motivation*:

> Flexibility: "The slightest adjustments to your daily routines can dramatically alter the outcomes in your life." —Darren Hardy

> Accomplishment: "It is not necessary to do extraordinary things to get extraordinary results." —Warren Buffett

> Desire: "Whether you think you can or think you can't, you're right." — Henry Ford

> Motivation: "Just keep swimming." —Dory (from *Finding Nemo*)

Successful leaders today draw from a similar reservoir of *purpose, intensity, confidence,* and *knowledge* that carries their goals and ambitions forward by applying them to the goals and objectives of the organizations they lead.

It is how innovative business leaders like Reed Hastings (Netflix), Jan Koum (WhatsApp), Elon Musk (Tesla Motors), Jeff Bezos (Amazon), and Warren Buffett (Berkshire Hathaway) advanced their organizations. Each of these leaders possesses these four qualities that drive them in their pursuit of success.

CASE IN POINT: WHATSAPP

WhatsApp was the brainchild of Jan Koum, a down-and-out computer programmer who had just walked away from nine years at Yahoo. His idea was to come about over the next two years while taking some time for himself and seeing the world with a friend who also needed a break.

After leaving Yahoo in 2007, he traveled within South America along with his future partner, Brian Acton, and then went on to Europe. What he learned from those travels was how difficult it was to keep in touch with friends, based on the different country codes and on not knowing who was available or when they were available to connect.

Based on the need he uncovered combined with his new iPhone, purchased in 2009, WhatsApp was born. His idea was to create an app that would allow individuals to connect with family and friends from anywhere in the world using their cellphone. Koum incorporated the idea on February 24, 2009.

His idea for a mobile app that connects individuals through messaging was an instant success, right? . . . wrong! WhatsApp1.0, as Koum put it, was, "A total failure: Nobody used it."[4] His purpose was to replace a "native dialer" by getting that person to text. His *intensity* was evidenced through the many conversations he had with Brian Acton, a computer engineer and internet entrepreneur, whom he convinced to join him as a co-founder two years later.

Koum first met Acton while working at Ernst & Young. Later the two ended up working together again at Yahoo for nine years. Their time at Yahoo furthered their *knowledge* of computer programming and allowed them to build trust in one another through a strong relationship that would serve them well in future years. Their combined *knowledge*, along with Koum's *intensity*, gave Koum the *confidence* needed to pursue his passion in developing the app.

His singular *purpose* is what drove him to connect individuals with the ability to communicate via text from anywhere in the world, providing they had access to a network and possession of a cell phone.

To say Koum's *purpose* was *intense* is an understatement. It became, in his own words, "An obsession"—referring to his quest to provide a solution that people needed to communicate versus becoming an entrepreneur with the intent of getting rich. "Koum thinks the word entrepreneurship is for people who create businesses to make money. He says it's more fitting for people who sold web companies in the 1990s and are now creating mobile apps. Koum says he just wanted to build a great product, not find wealth. He thinks it's 'silly' when people compare founders like himself to rock stars."[5]

That *intensity* and *confidence* sustained him in his quest over the next two years dealing with setbacks and failed attempts for the app to catch on until 2011, when "Apple released push notifications, which allowed WhatsApp to notify users once they had received a message. The app was adapted to become an instant messenger app where users would message contacts globally without any cost."[6] The culmination of Koum's *purpose, intensity, confidence,* and *knowledge* resulted in the sale of his company to Facebook in 2014, just five years after incorporating it for a reported $19 billion.

> The rise in popularity of messaging service WhatsApp has been nothing short of meteoric. The company was co-founded in 2009 by Jan Koum, and three years later it was processing 10 billion messages daily. In June 2013 WhatsApp proclaimed a new record of 27 billion messages handled in one day, and by the end of the year, the company declared that it had 400 million monthly users.[7]

Worth mentioning is the fact that Facebook rejected both Koum's and partner Brian Acton's application for employment seven years earlier.

The struggles Koum faced were real, and they were disappointing. Sheer will and determination drove him forward despite these challenges, which speaks to his *intensity*. It is the same intensity that drives any leader to achieve in the face of adversity and it is why this characteristic is so important for any leader determined to blaze their own trail.

Intensity is measured by our will, how committed we are to something through sheer desire, force, and potency. It is willpower, our control exerted over our desire, that keeps us focused and on track, driving us onward despite the setbacks or challenges we encounter; and that is precisely what kept Koum from abandoning his purpose: "To build a product that people used."[8]

As seasoned leaders, we all have stories of similar challenge and can recall times when we needed to push onward to stay the course and achieve our objectives. *Intensity* is what gives us the energy to keep on fighting for what we believe in, our purpose, and that is what all leaders need to have in order to address real challenges. Stories like Koum's give us inspiration to accomplish great things!

Inspiring articles make us think about new possibilities in ways that are transformative and transferable to situations we are encountering, or expect to come up against in the future as a leader. We are all living in a world that has seen centuries of invention, trial and error, and benefits to humanity in ways that seem impossible to top; however, the evolution of ideas based on needs never seem to end.

Mavericks and trailblazers exist in every department, company, or organization and it starts when leaders question the way something is or has been done and begin looking for a better way to do it, whether that be a change in policy, practice, or building a better "mouse trap."

A great blog to follow for any leader is Inspiring Leadership Now (ILN) at https://www.inspiringleadershipnow.com. Their focus on unwavering determination of innovative leaders based on their will to succeed is engaging and worth following. The creative minds behind ILN explain who they are by stating what they are about:

At Inspiring Leadership Now, we're fascinated by people who think a little differently. Those who have an innovative twinkle in their eye, or who are not afraid to break the mold of conventionality.

- Whether it be coming up with a seemingly outlandish concept . . .
- Having an empowering and unique leadership style . . .
- Developing a life-changing invention . . .
- Or creating a product that benefits the world around them . . . even if the world is yet to catch up to their way of thinking.

What makes these "leaders" so inspiring is that they decided to go ahead with their idea all guns blazing because something inside of them said, "Hang on, I think I might have something here."

And as a result of their unwavering determination to put these wheels in motion, they inspired others to follow them and contribute to their grander vision.

This, in our humble opinion, is the definition of an inspiring leader.

That is the magic of inspiration, moving others to action in ways that get results. When we apply creativity, thinking outside the "box" or better said, the "norm," we conceive of new pathways. Pathways that have yet to be discovered since they are our own, and these paths that we blaze can and will deliver our people to new destinations in ways that distinguish us from the competition, improve operations, and achieve success on a scale unimaginable. When we apply *purpose, intensity, confidence* and *knowledge* to our efforts, we become unstoppable as leaders and the scale to our achievement becomes limitless. These applied behaviors allow us to forge pathways where none exist in pursuit of our ideas as we blaze new trails for others to follow.

Chapter 5

Becoming EPIC (Energy, Purpose, Integrity, and Character)

Becoming epic is all about a story, a journey, and a hero. The hero/heroine must rise above their circumstance and leave the ordinary world to accept a call to action or great adventure by crossing the threshold into another world, a special world, where they will be tested, measured and, if found worthy—they will triumph.

The same is true in leadership with great leaders who become epic. It's a journey that takes time, discipline, resolve, and tenacity along with courage, guidance, bravery, and allies to defeat enemies, overcome obstacles, and meet the challenges that test us as we move toward the ultimate prize—self-actualization.

A hero's journey as detailed in Campbell's book, *The Hero's Journey,*[1] provides us with a structure that lays out the trip in three acts, making it applicable to any journey containing a hero or heroine that reaches the end by returning to the real world, dubbed "ordinary" by Campbell, with the prize, making them a legend and their story epic or legendary.

In leadership, our journeys contain the same degree of challenge—and setbacks will and do occur, but that's what elevates the journey beyond a mere trip, making it epic. But wait—unless we win the prize, capture the gold ring, or seize the reward, we cannot return as the hero but instead will suffer an epic defeat. It is the successful ending that dictates the telling and retelling of the story as we savor the victories that make our heroes epic.

Like so many of the words in use today, "epic" (16th-century Latin)[2] originated with the Greeks in the form of "epos" meaning word, song, that evolved from the ancient Greek adjective "epikos" or poetic story.

Merriam-Webster's Dictionary defines "epic" as 1: a long narrative poem in elevated style recounting the deeds of a legendary or historical hero;[3] 2: a work of art (such as a novel or drama) that resembles or suggests an epic;[4]

and 3: a series of events or body of legend or tradition thought to form the proper subject of an epic.[5]

As leaders, we need to think about everything we do as building towards an epic story of our own, one of courage, determination, and resolve. To get there we will need four things: **Energy, Purpose, Integrity,** and **Character.**

ENERGY

Becoming epic starts with the ability to generate energy from within. Energy is what powers our actions to engage in the activities we need to accomplish every day. If we don't have it, we are useless. If we don't have enough energy—things won't get done! Or they won't get done right.

Generating enough power for the loads we manage (career/family/community) requires control, motivation, determination, and goal setting.

Goals give us purpose. When we have a purpose, we find a reason for doing what needs to get done, as well as doing what we want to do. When we do what we want to do, we get excited, which generates energy, whereas doing what we have to do is often draining and uses up far more energy.

But what happens when that energy dissipates? Whenever our energy levels go down or get depleted we need to recharge our batteries and find ways to restore our power.

In the energy industry the focus is on renewable sources of energy to ensure we have enough energy to meet our needs: "To heat our houses, power our cities and run our cars."[6] Renewable energy sources are cleaner and healthier for the environment. As a result, they are healthier for the planet and those who inhabit it.

The same is true for individuals. When it comes to finding sources of renewable energy to keep us powered up and enjoying healthier, more productive lives, we need to tap into available resources as well as find new sources that are sustainable and plentiful.

In our busy world, leaders need to tap into energy sources that generate power to take on challenges, brainstorm solutions, and roll up their sleeves to dig into the work that has to be done, even if that means managing the effort.

While leading does not always equate to doing—as leaders we remain responsible to ensure the work is getting done, and getting done right.

That takes a high degree of energy to not only come up with solutions to problems, but seeing those solutions carried out, recorded, communicated, reviewed, approved, and documented.

In June 2016, Harvard Health published nine tips to boost your energy—naturally.[7] Harvard Health Publishing (HHP) is the consumer health education division of Harvard Medical School (HMS). Their publications are cultivated from the real-life experiences and expertise of the 11,000+ faculty physicians at HMS, as well as their world-famous affiliated hospitals. As such, their publications ensure trust and expert advice, and provide actionable health information to a global audience.

The article referenced above reported on ways to get more energy, including stress relief and healthy eating, to include: *controlling stress, lightening your load, exercising, avoiding smoking, restricting sleep, eating properly, benefits/drawbacks of caffeine, limiting alcohol, and drinking water.*[8]

In education, we talk about deep diving to conduct a closer inspection to gain a deeper understanding of something. So while the article addresses the subject matter in a general health advisement way, let's look at applying the first three tips to our settings as managers and leaders to raise our energy levels:

Tip 1. Controlling Stress—*Practical Application:* Identify what your stressors are by examining your challenges (people, schedules, workload, etc.) and then plan ways to meet those challenges and reduce or embrace the stress.

Certain stress (eustress) is actually beneficial and helps us to meet challenges in a way that energizes us to tackle them. Negative stress; however, can not only be harmful, it zaps energy faster than anything when emotions come into play. Think about emergencies and how drained we are once they end. Exhaustion sets in as our bodies come out of "overdrive" from generating the "fight-or-flight" chemicals that release to deal with the emergency.

There is also a direct link between power and stress in leadership—the more power we possess, the more stress we inherit. Again the challenge is to manage that stress by converting it into positively charged energy that powers our progress; therefore igniting our passion which thrusts us towards victory, versus the negative energy that leaves us sluggish, disconnected, and defeated.

Jennifer Jordan, a social psychologist and professor of Leadership and Organizational Behavior at the Institute for Management Development in Switzerland wrote an article focused on the importance of personal energy and how to manage that energy. The article references the work of Francesca Giulia Mereu, utilizing her concept of energy being broken down into four dimensions: physical, emotional, mental, and spiritual.[9]

Patterned after batteries, each cell is interrelated, which allows you to deplete one or more while charging the others depending on the task at hand, which may require more mental effort than physical, for example.

"Learning to manage your energy will help you sustain and increase your performance and quality of life and reduce your stress, which in turn will help you be a stronger and more effective leader."[10]

Recharging not only revitalizes us, it helps us manage our energy levels to become more effective as leaders. Recharging is a topic I will discuss at length in the next chapter.

Tip 2. Lightening your load—*Practical Application:* As the HHP article points out, "Try to streamline your list of 'must-do' activities. Set your priorities in terms of the most important tasks. Pare down those that are less important. Consider asking for extra help at work, if necessary."

"Look at your projects and tasks, and order them by deadline. Ask yourself: What can I stop doing, do less of, or do more efficiently?"

For example, you may be generating reports and creating spreadsheets for an analysis of account balances when your boss just wants to know the status of a particular receipt. In this case too much time is wasted preparing information that is not relevant to the request. This self-created work adds to the workload and keeps individuals from completing other, more relevant tasks that need their attention.

In counseling colleagues and supervisors regarding workload, apply a common-sense approach to determining capacity of work by sharing the philosophy of *working smarter, not harder*. If you work smarter, you find ways to accomplish tasks quicker, without wasting energy on needless steps or work that doesn't matter since it is not necessary to accomplish the task.

Try these simple tricks to reduce time spent "re-creating" work:

- Build templates to tackle future projects of similar types
- Convert, retrofit, or re-engineer systems, processes, or reports to adapt to changing needs
- Avoid going too far from the original task, don't get lost in the weeds
- Make notes to provide a trail for yourself and others to avoid lost time to unnecessary research in the future. trying to figure out how and why you got here
- Look at applying "best practices" by reaching out to colleagues to see if anyone has experience with issues you are dealing with or ones you may encounter down the road

Working smarter, not harder is about focusing on what's important and what has to be done. We do this by prioritizing tasks and ensuring we have both the capacity and capability to ensure good outcomes.

Tip 3. Exercise—*Practical Application:* Just do it. While the article points out the benefits of exercise related to sleeping better and energy, studies have proven, "The amount of energy you have is a direct result of your diet and the number of mitochondria your body produces."[11]

Article after article speaks to the benefits of exercise, and any leader who has made it a part of their routine can attest to the immediate and plentiful benefits related to energy. It gives you the added benefit of controlling your workout, selecting personal goals, letting go of stress, and clearing your head by processing events that have taken place or gearing up for what lies ahead.

While Nike advises us to "Just d-o i-t!"[12], the company name is founded on the Greek word meaning *victory* and that's how we feel when we meet our workout goals.

PURPOSE

Purpose is what that drives us onward in any quest and it is *purpose* that keeps us moving along the path toward becoming epic. Purpose gives us the energy needed to complete the journey, regardless of the distance we need to go or the terrain we need to traverse. Absent purpose, we have no reason. Without reason, we lose direction and start to wander. When we wander we stray further from the goals we set for ourselves and those we set for our organizations.

It is purpose that provides meaning in our work and our deeds. As a result, they become impactful, relevant, and beneficial. When they are recounted by others, they take on grander scope and size, synonymous with words like: outstanding, excellent, or impressive.

An article titled "From Purpose to Impact" appeared in the *Harvard Business Review* in May 2014,[13] in which the writers noted a surge in interest surrounding "purpose driven leadership" in organizations.

The writers share, "Training thousands of managers at organizations from GE to the Girl Scouts, and teaching an equal number of executives and students at Harvard Business School, we've found that fewer than 20% of leaders have a strong sense of their own individual purpose. Even fewer can distill their purpose into a concrete statement."

> Think of Google's "To organize the world's information and make it universally accessible and useful," or Charles Schwab's "A relentless ally for the individual investor." But when asked to describe their own purpose, they typically fall back on something generic and nebulous: "Help others excel." "Ensure success." "Empower my people." Just as problematic, hardly any of them have a clear plan for translating purpose into action. As a result, they limit their aspirations and often fail to achieve their most ambitious professional and personal goals.[14]

Lacking purpose not only limits our potential as leaders, it prevents us from serving others in ways that are beneficial, meaningful, or remembered.

When a leader's purpose focuses on serving their own interests over that of their teams, organizations, and stakeholders, they are quickly forgotten and seldom spoken about as most people try to stay positive especially in public—they will never be epic, as their story will never be told.

In the closing paragraph of the article, the question is raised, "What creates the greatest leaders and companies?" The response is excellent advice with respect to making our purpose actionable:

> Each of them operates from a slightly different set of assumptions about the world, their industry, what can or can't be done. That individual perspective allows them to create great value and have significant impact. They all operate with a unique leadership purpose. To be a truly effective leader, you must do the same. Clarify your purpose, and put it to work.[15]

INTEGRITY

Leaders who become epic are those who lead in ways that never compromise the virtues of doing the right thing, especially during a crisis, facing a challenge, or confronting a hardship, where compromise—although easy, is not acceptable—at least not to them.

As a leader, *integrity* is an *all-or-nothing* proposition—you either have it or you don't. Anything less than 100% calls your actions into question, weakens your authority, hurts your team, and damages your reputation.

Strong moral principles help guide our decisions as leaders to ensure we have the best interests of our people (teams, organizations, clients, stakeholders) at heart.

Draped in a cloak of honesty, we engage those we encounter with a visible sense of honor, respect, and incorruptibility, tied to a code of morality and ethics.

In business it means we carry out each transaction in a way that maintains our code of conduct in an ethical and principled way regardless of the terms set and agreed upon. We do not shy away from addressing what is wrong but instead fight for what is right, just, and fair.

Integrity is what separates good leaders from bad leaders; however, leaders who are successful in acquiring, maintaining, and displaying integrity during their toughest trials are those who become legendary as their deeds become epic and their stories are told and retold.

NPR (National Public Radio) ran a two-minute segment on February 20, 2012 about the over 15,000 books on Abraham Lincoln, declaring him, "Second only to Jesus Christ as the most written about person in history of the world."[16] The books have been arranged in an impressive tower standing

34 feet tall and 8 feet around, surrounded by a spiral staircase in the lobby of Ford's Theatre in Washington, D.C.

While Lincoln is recognized for many of his leadership traits, it was his uncompromising integrity that garnered respect from all who encountered him, including his foes and those who witnessed his resolve in preserving the Union through the bloodiest battle in the history of our nation.

A quick blurb from Reference.com summed it up with this quote:

> President Lincoln is lauded for his integrity, particularly regarding his management of the Civil War. All his decisions sprang from his belief that maintaining the American form of government, as expressed through the Union, was vital. His refusal to deal with dishonest people was just an extension of that natural integrity.[17]

But that was then, and we are here more than 150 years later—so what's the point? What can we learn from leaders such as Lincoln, Gandhi, Martin Luther King Jr., and others who pushed the boundaries of what "was" to change things into how they "should be?"

It is the fact that without integrity, they would not have succeeded in bringing their vision to life by incorporating the support of others to fulfill a dream of equality (MLK), obtain freedom through non-violence (Gandhi), and save the Union (Lincoln).

As leaders, *integrity is as important today* as it was in their time. Without it we cannot guide, we cannot lead, we cannot succeed. Our teams, our organizations, our companies, and our communities depend on leaders to do what's right. When they don't, it breaks the public trust and damages the credibility of those leaders, sometimes irreparably.

Stakeholders expect leaders to do what is in the best interest of the groups they manage, not their own.

People choose to follow leaders they believe in because they believe those leaders can accomplish the goals they share in or allow them to achieve the victories they seek. As long as things go well, it is easy to follow them, and when we prosper as a result of their leadership, it's easy to stay loyal.

Charismatic leaders are great at motivating and building a following that sparks immediate interest, energy, and desire. However, absent integrity, those feelings are diminished, and the movement becomes short-lived.

"Employees will forgive and forget a leader's errors in judgment, but they will never forget his lack of integrity."[18]

CHARACTER

When it comes to an epic story involving character, we need look no further than the immortal number 42—the first African American to play in Major League Baseball in the modern era. Jackie Robinson broke the baseball color line when he started at first base for the Brooklyn Dodgers on April 15, 1947.[19]

> Jackie Robinson's life and legacy will be remembered as one of the most important in American history. In 1997, the world celebrated the 50th Anniversary of Jackie's breaking Major League Baseball's color barrier. In doing so, we honored the man who stood defiantly against those who would work against racial equality and acknowledged the profound influence of one man's life on the American culture. On the date of Robinson's historic debut, all Major League teams across the nation celebrated this milestone. Also that year, The United States Post Office honored Robinson by making him the subject of a commemorative postage stamp.[20]

What made Jackie Robinson's story epic is the way in which he developed, maintained, and displayed character. That character is what set him apart from many of his peers on the field and on other teams in the league who were just as blessed with raw talent, personality, and a love for the game. It is character that immortalized his contributions to humanity and grabbed the attention of a nation at a time when racism was pervasive.

His story, being epic, was retold again on April 9, 2013, with the release of the film *42,* starring another "great" with epic character, Chadwick Boseman, playing the immortal Robinson. The film grossed $97.5 million on a production budget of $40 million.[21] For audiences new to the story, it demonstrated the power of character to withstand the trials that most individuals, given the same set of circumstances, would have given in.

The Foundation for a Better Life, a nonprofit offering public service announcements, seized on Robinson's character in a recent billboard campaign urging others to take the values expressed by Robinson in the form of "Character" and "Pass It On!" Their website not only captures Robinson's contribution but provides a platform for all leaders who want to make a difference in their own stories on the road to becoming epic heroes while leading their teams and organization in ways that benefit society as a whole—that's epic:

> But in addition to being a phenomenal athlete, Robinson was a pioneer, a hero, and a representative of many values that continue to inspire us today. He stands as a true example of innovation and foresight, based in the strength of character to achieve any goal you can imagine.[22]

While writing this chapter, I bounced my ideas off a colleague who jumped up at the title and said, "OMG that's a T-Shirt!" Her enthusiasm for the acronym was instant gratification and assured me I was on to something; however, her next words set me back a bit as the question she posed made me think: *"What is the distinction between character and integrity?"* Not only was it a good question, it sent me on a quest to define both in a way that encapsulates the essence of leadership for both that form separate elements of an epic storyline.

The placement of *Integrity* before *Character* resulted in hitting on the acronym I came up with and truth be told, it was serendipitous. Why did I start with integrity? Because as leaders, without integrity we have no code, no moral compass, we do not stand for anything, or at least nothing good or nothing of value.

Without integrity we can never develop the type of character needed to lead. *Merriam-Webster's Dictionary* defines character as, "attributes or features that make up and distinguish an individual."[23] But character, unlike integrity, takes years to build as it is defined by our actions in the face of adversity.

Character does not come from a life of ease and comfort where everything is given freely or provided without effort, but one in which we struggle, face adversity, and rise up to meet the challenges before us without *giving in* or *compromising our values.*

"Anyone can hold the helm when the sea is calm."[24] The quote is all about *character* because it is *character* that is required to take the helm during any storm when the ship and crew are in peril, facing the risk of being injured, destroyed, or lost. The quote comes to us from a Latin writer, Publilius Syrus (fl. 85–43 BC),[25] a Syrian from Antioch who had his own adversity to overcome. He was brought as a slave to Roman Italy, but it was his wit and talent that won his freedom and education.[26]

Throughout history, trials and tribulations were character-building opportunities, and those who triumphed over adversity typically went on to accomplish incredible feats, with some becoming legendary and their stories epic.

In the end, character is what takes the longest time to develop since it must be built one experience at a time and tested many times to forge our mettle as leaders.

Most of us will never face the dragon or pull the sword from the stone on our journeys, but we all have our own Rubicons to cross like Julius Caeser, changing the fate of Rome forever. How you deal with your challenges will set your fate, to be sure. As leaders we are challenged every day, but some challenges define us as heroic due to the sheer magnitude of the challenge, the personal cost of the victory, and the benefit to others—making us epic

Chapter 6

The Difference Between Courage and Recklessness

Some leaders, especially those who are new to leadership, mistake reckless abandon (rash, unrestrained impulsiveness, or zeal) for courage by throwing themselves into a cause at the cost of personal peril. This avoidance chapter focuses on what not to do as a new leader concerning fighting for a cause. Don't lose everything by fighting for everything! Yet, understand there is a time to fight, and we need to distinguish when that time is and prepare for battle when that time is at hand.

As written in Ecclesiastes 3:8[1], there is a time to every purpose under the heaven: A time to love, and a time to hate; a time of war, and a time of peace. This lesson was popularized by the band, the Bryds with their song, "Turn! Turn! Turn! (To Everything There Is a Season)."[2]

The sayings, "It is never the wrong time to do the right thing!" (attributed to Mark Twain), and "The time is always right to do what is right!" (proclaimed by Dr. King), challenge mankind to be better, to be courageous, and to be accountable for their actions. Good advice for anyone; however, required advice for leaders intent on becoming difference makers.

But it comes at a price, and that price can be steep at times, involving personal sacrifice, which could in some cases put careers on the line. The question is not whether the cause you are fighting for is worth it, but whether or not you need to risk everything in pursuit of it.

Make no mistake, we are not talking about "championing an idea" like Koums and Acton in chapter 4 with the creation of WhatsApp. In this chapter, the stakes are much higher (career, integrity, and honor), and the takeaway is about knowing *how to achieve your objectives without compromising your career*. Avoiding what I like to call your "*Braveheart* moment" – you don't want to be yelling "FREEDOM!" while you're being drawn and quartered as a result of achieving that objective.

Another way to put it: *You don't want to pick a hill to die on!* This idiom describes something you see as so important that you are willing to die for it, giving your life to achieve it, or more likely willing to sacrifice your career if you lose.

> The phrase is often used in a question: Is this the hill you want to die on? This question may be considered a warning that taking a certain stance will probably result in defeat of one sort or another. The idiom *the hill you want to die on* is derived from a military term. Fighting to take the position of a hill from an enemy is nearly impossible and results in mass casualties. One must be sure that the hill is worth the cost of taking it.[3]

As new leaders and even experienced leaders who might have forgotten, you need to learn the value of *negotiations* and *compromise*. Not every battle needs to be fought and not every battle that is fought will be won. You need to learn the difference and measure the cost to determine what is worth fighting for—choosing your battles and being prepared to fight makes all the difference.

Throughout history, preparation has made the difference in waging and fighting wars, and those wars are not just reserved for the battlefield. Business is and can be just as dangerous as we navigate through minefields in every industry, organization, and company in which we are deployed. This requires us to suit up every day in our own armor of *strategic thought, deliberate action,* and *intense awareness* to navigate the terrain while dealing with threats from situations and people intent on stopping us from achieving our objectives.

If you think it's war—you're right! If it's a war you want, you got it! But every war requires tactics and strategies to win, and it's not always over in one swift battle. Many objectives require months or even years of planning, problem solving, team building, and political maneuvering to come out on top and then stay there. Planting the flag is one thing, defending it is another.

Robert Greene wrote *The 33 Strategies of War* to help you win in business, breaking them down into five types of warfare: Self-Directed Warfare, Organizational (Team) Warfare, Defensive Warfare, Offensive Warfare, and Unconventional (Dirty) Warfare.[4]

While his points are made and some have serious merit, Genghis Khan is not who I want to be!

A bit Machiavellian, many of the strategies are on point provided one accepts the moral belief, "the end justifies the means." I'm not so sure that this is always the case; however, it does change one's perspective. Keep in mind "war" is "war" and we are not at war—but we are dealing with people who work against us, want the same things we want, and are willing to do many things that we are not. What is important as a leader is what you believe in and what you stand for that makes you principled.

A close friend once told me, "Don't mistake my kindness for weakness." He runs a critical department involving varied team members with exceptional skill sets and he interacts with executives and community leaders at many levels. What makes him so successful is that he understands people and understands what they are capable of; however, he maintains his decorum and personal standards in every situation. Basically, the guy is not for sale—he stands his ground—even when punching above his weight class because he knows how to compromise in coming to an effective solution without compromising who he is as a leader and what he stands for.

So how do we go from *compassion* as outlined in chapter 3 as one of the Top Ten characteristics for leaders, to *combat* which is all about conflict? We start by first realizing *life is challenging* and *people are people* and they don't always think the way you do; however, as leaders we need to convince them to support us in our endeavors or *conquer them in the process*. If we fail to win the day or take the ground, we may regroup to fight another day, but if we lose *too often* or *too big*, we may be out—out of time, out of the competition, or out of a job.

This means persuasion, influence and other means of attracting, motivating, and gaining support on your quest, but sometimes it means battles or even war.

Greene's strategies are based on knowledge; knowledge of ourselves (Self-Directed Warfare), knowledge of our teams (Organizational Warfare), knowledge of our enemies (Defensive/Offensive Warfare), and knowledge of covert activities designed to promote unrest and unseat those in power.

The last category, Unconventional Warfare, which Green categorizes as "dirty" warfare, need not corrupt who we are as leaders, nor should it reflect the principles we believe in as leaders. Instead, we need to realize that these tactics do exist and that we need to prepare to defend against them as well as conceive of acceptable ways to counter them.

Adopting clever plans to surprise our enemies with a stratagem designed to gain an advantage over our competitors is simply good business strategy. When a leader plays dirty, they get dirty; more often than not, that dirt stains in ways that cannot be cleaned, especially when it is not in keeping with our moral or ethical code of conduct. But "bad actors" are out there and you need to beware, be ready. and be willing to fight against them.

Remember these are individuals (rivals) who will stop at nothing to extinguish your flame or block your path in hopes of getting there ahead of you, whether that be a discovery, recognition for your efforts on a project, a promotion, or even jockeying for a coveted position in your company or a competitor's.

Growing up, we trained for these situations when playing board games that reward strategy by holding back our intent until we took our turn to dominate and wipe out the competition, which in this case was family and friends. Classics like chess, Risk, Monopoly, and Clue brought out our competitive side—and who hasn't ended one of the family game nights with someone crying as they hit Boardwalk and went broke while someone else is raking in the money before the board gets flipped and everyone is sent to bed?

So how do we become *warrior leaders* when the time comes to fight the battles we need to fight? By rallying our troops and pushing back the advances of our enemies, defending our teams, defeating our enemies, and advancing our units, our companies, and our organizations. This in turn advances our careers and improves our skills as leaders to thwart off future threats, all the while blazing new trails to be the first one to do something and to show others how to do it—that is the essence of leading.

This can all be accomplished by invoking these **10 Rules to Surviving Battles**:

Rule 1: Protect Your Team and Protect Yourself—In basic training we learned the importance of "move and cover" to conceal and protect our advancement on an enemy position. That basic military rule of the battlefield is transferable to our civilian work environments. Advancing without the protection of cover puts anyone at risk of being shot by a sniper (hidden enemy) or taken out by a force (group enemy); either way you're hit, injured, or worse. Taking cover is not hiding but merely protecting us from enemy fire and allowing us to assess our situation while we await the next part of the exercise, moving toward our target. Concealment allows us to hold that position longer.

In our organizations it means looking out for your team and having them look out for you by keeping abreast of what's happening and staying a step ahead by recognizing the Strengths, Weaknesses, Opportunities and Threats (SWOT) afoot within your organization. It means knowing what is needed to achieve the goals and objectives of the organization and having your team(s) in lockstep with those goals.

IGYB (-I Got Your Back) is looking out for members of your team who in turn look out for you and, trust me, it matters. It conveys three critical elements of fortification: "I support you." "I'm here for you." "I will protect you." It strengthens our teams and our position within that organization.

Rule 2: Protect Your Work—Safeguarding your work, strategies, and initiatives is all about making them bulletproof before presenting or advancing them within or outside of our organizations. While in process, that work is the most vulnerable, since ideas are not owned and the work product itself is in the draft stage. It is at risk of being taken, held hostage to other initiatives, or destroyed at the expense of other, competing interests.

The strategy of "Creating a sense of urgency and desperation" shared by Greene,[5] that is, -"Place yourself where your back is against the wall and you have to fight like hell to get out alive"[6] is an essential one. Once adopted, this strategy helps to ensure we are "on -it!" and that our work is compelling and-thus worthy of the resources being allocated to its continuation.

Rule 3: District First (Company or Organization)—District First refers to the organization in which I serve, and those I have belonged to over the past 24 years. The rule is one I live by, going back to my time as a board member in Lincoln Park, New Jersey. I impress it upon my staff, district supervisors, principals, and administrators, along with colleagues and those I have mentored over the years. It is simple, yet effective in avoiding and winning fights concerning what we should and should not be doing, supporting, or approving.

Every action should come down to what's in the best interest of the district. Here are some examples:

- Leave—Is the approval of an individual's request for leave (outside of what is required by law versus permitted by contract upon mutual agreement) in the best interest of the district, or simply their own?
- Travel—Does attendance at a requested workshop or conference by an employee provide value for the district?
- Stipends/Extra-Pay/Overtime—Does the benefit we receive as a district outweigh the added expense or cost of the service provided? Or is this just an attempt to boost someone's paycheck?

The point is, regardless of the decisions you are faced with, and whether or not you manage a school district, a Fortune 500 Company, or a nonprofit, you need to make good decisions. Whenever people have access to resources, equipment, money, or intellectual property, you need to consider the beneficiaries in the exchange or transaction and if the company is not one of them, then you should not be approving the request.

If the decision you are contemplating pertains to you personally—the same rule applies and will undoubtedly keep you out of trouble!

Rule 4: Know and Understand the Competition—Being aware of the competition means all competition inside and outside of the organization. Competitors are all around us, this is a fact, and if you do not realize this fact, you will be left standing on the sidelines of life.

To do this, to achieve maximum awareness, we need to be aware of our surroundings at all times, even in social situations when we interact with colleagues and co-workers who in many cases become and remain our competition while preparing to lead. Social settings allow for networking and maneuvering and can be used to your advantage.

Recognizing who is who, and being able to discern between friend and foe, is critical to navigating minefields and avoiding traps. Individuals who "work the room" are adept at communicating, and more importantly, listening as they gather information to gain better perspectives on what others think, uncover their intentions, and learn what they perceive to be important concerning needs, expectations, and desires.

Excelling at this skill allows leaders and future leaders to build a rapport with opinion leaders, bosses and future bosses, and power brokers/influencers while gaining insights, finding common ground, and gaining ground over rivals.

Greene categorizes this strategy under Offensive Warfare, summarized in a 2014 article that appeared in *Business Insider* magazine as, "Pay less attention to the entire team of your competition and instead study its leader. Avoid projecting your beliefs onto that person, instead observing how he or she thinks and behaves."[7]

Keep in mind this can all be accomplished with the elements of leading described in the opening of this part of the book, "Leading with Purpose, Integrity, Confidence, and Knowledge," as it is an opportunity to elicit support from volunteers and gain converts to your team, allowing you to gain more influence.

Understanding how to work with others in support of their goals the same way you need their support to achieve your goals is just plain smart. However, when pursuing the same goal—a promotion, a new position, landing a new account, or whatever your aim, and there can be only one (reminds me of *Highlander*—another great movie), you need to ensure you are bringing the skills, drive, ambition, and desire to win to achieve that goal and beat out the competition. This includes keeping some things close to the vest, allowing you to retain original ideas by avoiding "overshare" or tipping off the competition to your plans or your progress in pursuit of mutual goals.

Another strategy outlined in Greene's *33 Strategies of War* is a familiar military strategy: "Divide a-nd -Conquer" or in his case, "Defeat them in detail,"[8] referring to breaking down a challenger or challenge into smaller, more easily defeated parts. This fits nicely within this rule of "Know and Understand the Competition" since you need to see *what* and *who* you are up against to develop strategies to outplay, outwit, and outthink competitors.

"In division there is weakness. The two things we take from this is to be wary of being divided ourselves as individuals, as groups, and to understand that the best way to fight an enemy is to divide them first."[9]

Going deeper yet, consider "defeating in detail" to mean *defeating with detail*, leaving no stone unturned concerning the level of detail that we arm ourselves with in preparation for the battles we need to fight. The action strategy of *detail preparation* allows us to draw from an arsenal of weaponry that improves our range while engaging targets and just may avoid some unnecessary "hand-to-hand" combat.

Rule 5: Trust but Verify and Need to Know—Start by limiting that trust to only those who have earned it. It is ok to trust or give people the benefit of the doubt on low-level/low-impact jobs/projects, assignments, and general work. Verification that the tasks or work is being completed allows leaders to gain confidence in the ability of their teams while at the same time increasing that trust for higher level/high-impact jobs/projects, assignments, and highly technical work.

The first part of this rule comes from the immortal words of Ronald Reagan, borrowed from a Russian proverb he came upon while preparing for disarmament talks with then Russian leader Mikhail Gorbachev in the late 1980s. Its meaning (the proverb) is that a responsible person always verifies everything before committing himself to a common business with anyone, even if that anyone is totally trustworthy.[10]

Many of us have heard the sage advice from those closest to us in life, like a parent, a close relative, or a mentor, who impart words of concern for us, saying things like "Don't be too trusting!" or "You have a tendency to trust too quickly." In these two cases and many others related to the caution, we are simply being warned in order to avoid being hurt, taken advantage of, or cheated. This doesn't mean we should not trust people, nor does it mean trust cannot be earned. It just means you should not trust blindly or without good cause.

But trust is necessary in all aspects of our lives including our work, our relationships, and our organizations. As leaders we need to develop trust, extend trust, and manage trust in order to accomplish our missions, push the boundaries of what is possible, and explore new opportunities, all synonymous with trailblazing. The quicker we achieve trust, the quicker we attain our goals with less expense as proven by Stephen Covey in his work, *The Speed of Trust*: "Trust is the new currency of our interdependent, collaborative world."[11]

So not only is it ok to trust, it is necessary, and we need to do it—just check the results of that trust.

The second part of this rule, "Need to Know," stems from the military, referring to information that should only be seen by those who need to know what it contains. Keeping sensitive, critical, or confidential matters protected from unnecessary or unauthorized disclosure starts with proper handling, and that means less handling or more specifically, fewer eyes on it. By restricting access, we limit the ability to compromise the information. In the world of military intelligence this rule falls under Operations Security or OPSEC. In our world, it falls under common sense.

Rule 6: Everything Is Negotiable, Everything—The key to surviving any skirmish is to be prepared, and that takes training, training, and more training—but you need to have a plan, execute that plan flawlessly, and gain the ground that matters—your objective(s).

But, as explained in the opening, *not every battle takes place on the battle-field, and not every fight requires heavy fighting* resulting in mass casualties (time, money, market share, etc.)—basically any advantage.

So how do we achieve this aim? Through negotiations, and as the rule states—everything is negotiable, everything: time, money, terms and conditions, benefits, hours of operations, policies, practices, budgets, freight charges, fines . . . I think you get the point.

"Never forget that in a negotiation, the other side is trying to take as much as possible from you that they could not get from direct confrontation. Before and during negotiations, keep your agenda moving forward so that your opponent plays on your terms."[12]

Negotiation allows us to gain steady ground with each round in the case of recurring contracts, or one-offs (single incidents), providing we have the courage and intelligence to avoid unnecessary battles and the knowledge, cunning, and insight to *fight small* and *win big* without getting bloodied or giving up too much ground in the exchange. Masters of negotiations know how to win and how to walk away with humility, respect, and appreciation for what they have achieved without infuriating the other party or parties.

Rule 7: Learn the Terrain and Map the Minefields—Understanding our environments means getting the "lay of the land"—knowing where the dangers are and how best to avoid them. Securing knowledge of the obstacles within our organizations and developing strategies to navigate them comes down to a decision: evade or attack.

Avoidance keeps us safe and free from harm as long as it remains possible and we keep from being careless or reckless. However, when you need to attack for your survival, you need to go at it like those competing on *American Ninja Warrior* (*ANW*).[13] In each season since its debut in 2009, the challengers study the courses they will encounter in each city on the path to Las Vegas in hopes of becoming that season's "American Ninja Warrior." That requires study and preparation to handle the obstacles that increase in difficulty until they reach the final destination.

Knowing what to look out for in our journeys is important to our survival, and knowing where the landmines are is how we prolong our careers; mapping their locations allows us to avoid stepping on and into explosive situations or encountering dangerous people who can cause harm, derail our efforts, or simply short circuit our careers, even for short periods.

As mentors, it allows us to point others in the right direction and share our knowledge of the landmines to guide them on the appropriate detour to protect their careers as well. Likewise, mapping the danger zones allows us to brief our teams in ways that build trust, confidence in our leadership, and appreciation for the team.

When we cannot avoid those situations and see no way out but through the minefield, then we fight with the support of our team(s) in disarming those landmines by knowing where they are and applying our knowledge of them to defuse them, again gaining valuable ground as we blaze new trails and prepare to take on the challenges quickly and decisively, bringing to bear all our force, knowledge, and training to take the ground and win the day.

Rule 8: Speak Up and Speak Out—Saying nothing says it's ok, and when it isn't, we need to speak up and speak out. How we do this and how our point is made can be the difference between stating our position and gaining respect, or looking for a new job—- again referring to being reckless.

As part of your defensive strategy, consider creating a threatening presence to keep your opponents and others from engaging you. By speaking up when challenged, mistreated, or overlooked and speaking out when others are treated badly, you display courage. Courage informs others you are willing to fight, and sometimes that is enough to get them to back down and avoid fighting. Not only does this aid in our survival, but it also gains respect and strengthens our team, forging a deeper bond of loyalty.

Controlling your message and *overwhelming resistance with speed and suddenness*[14] puts us back on offense and allows us to *maneuver our opponents into weakness*[15] by exposing their shortcomings. Strategic thinking allows us to become strategic speakers and therefore avoid reckless behavior and using inappropriate language that only hurts our position.

Rule 9: Identify What Matters—Focusing on what matters concentrates our actions and directs our efforts, but it also allows us to consider what is worth fighting for in the first place and how committed to that fight we need to be in the second.

If we argue over everything and lash out whenever something new comes down from above in a directive, memo, or change in practice, we will be seen as an agitator or obstructionist and certainly not as a leader.

One of the stories that exemplifies this is the advice Lincoln gave a young officer he came upon engaged in a quarrel. He said, "Quarrel not at all. No man resolved to make the most of himself, can spare time for personal contention. . . . Better to give your path to a dog, than be bitten by him in contesting for the right. Even killing the dog would not cure the bite."[16] That advice is now over a century and a half old, 157 years to be exact, and it still delivers the message that speaks to the rule.

When we choose our battles and learn the art of compromise we can more often than not find ways to implement the changes and satisfy the requirements in a way befitting our role as a leader.

Rule 10: Believe in Your Cause—When you believe in a cause, others will follow you as long as you remain committed to pursuing that cause. Passion inspires people, and nothing rallies people like supporting a great cause. When we believe in our cause, we are far more likely to defend that cause, regardless of the risks. The same goes for those aiding that cause.

That means we are committed to the fight, bringing energy, determination, and heart, making us unstoppable. As a force to be reckoned with, our chance for survival soars, and we become an imposing threat to our enemies.

So what does survival have in common with victory and defeat? The answer ends this chapter just as it began: It is possible to achieve survival in both scenarios as long as we think and act strategically and abide by these rules. Whenever we are victorious, we survive at least for that battle; however, in defeat, we can still survive, if only to heal, recover, and fight again another day. It is reckless abandon that should concern us most, as we need to ensure we are not fighting a losing battle to the point of no return, for then we may not recover and all is lost.

The easiest way to survive a fight is to know how to fight; the best way to win a fight is not to start one. However, when you find yourself in a fight over a cause you believe matters—consider the cause, consider the stakes, and apply the strategies that give you the best chance of winning or the good sense to negotiate the best compromise.

PART III

Pacesetters

Chapter 7

Recharging and Finding Balance

Recharging by definition is all about restoring power—as a verb, it conveys an action, occurrence, or state of being. Not only is it necessary, but it is also required to maintain the energy needed to tackle some of our biggest challenges as leaders. Recharging is all about finding peace, joy, and relaxation to return us to our top performance levels and get us through the new challenges and demands awaiting us in our busy lives.

The military refers to it as "R&R," an abbreviation for "rest and recuperation" or "rest and relaxation."[1] Ask any soldier and they can tell you "R&R" equates to "free time" and, trust me, it's a place they all want to go.

The U.S. travel iIndustry, working harder than ever to bounce back from the crippling impact of COVID-19 on travel, could not agree more with their newest campaign launched in March of 2021—*Let's Go There.*[2] Promoting the need for travel against the backdrop of COVID-19, the coalition incorporated the following message: "When It's Time for You, We'll Be Ready—Let's Go There," into a neatly designed logo.[3]

Due to COVID-19, 2020 became the lost year for many things including travel, vacation, and rest or relaxation for many, especially leaders who found themselves scrambling to maintain their businesses, protect their workers and customers, navigate funding assistance plans and payroll protection programs, and sourcing personal protective equipment (PPE) along with materials like Plexiglass. Add to this the personal toll, with over 144.7 million people worldwide[4] infected with the virus by April 23, 2021, and the number of deaths totalling more than 3 million.[5]

For a majority of managers and executives this meant dealing with the fallout of the pandemic or added pressures associated with remote management, over-reliance on video conferencing, and lost opportunities for in-person professional development. All of this meant longer hours and longer time spent managing the challenges associated with the crisis.

This time away from work meant you were still near work because the home office became the primary place of work. Time off, including official time off such as vacation, meant staying put or 'staycations." This resulted in more time spent in and around the confines of our homes, since travel was restricted.

Staycations can be nice at times; however, they miss the mark regarding restorative properties for recharging if they are the only source of our breaks. This happens because we are forced to stay in our surroundings and lose out on the discovery of something new and exciting.

Often staycations become more work in and around the house, which is fine provided we have given ourselves the breaks we need throughout the year that include getaways. "Everyone needs time away to unwind—and yes, that includes managers. Though managers may have a wealth of responsibilities and employees to take care of, the benefits of taking time off far outweigh the drawbacks."[6]

Managers and other leaders often cite "time" as a reason for not taking vacation days along with "too much work" to leave. The truth is—*time*, or in this case, PTO (paid time off), is more available for this group on average than for most employees in any organization. Accruing or earning vacation at the management level becomes easier over time as most leaders enjoy a healthy bank of vacation days for needed breaks or vacations.

The problem facing many of these leaders is not the inability to earn the benefit, but a problem with taking the benefit to relax, recharge, and return— fresh and focused to take on greater challenges.

A 2014 survey reported, "While 96 percent of Americans recognize the value of vacation days, over 40 percent don't use them."[7]

The 2018 *Report on the State of American Vacation* found that American workers accumulated 705 million unused days in 2017, up from 662 million days the year before.[8]

The same report issued by the U.S. Travel Association showed Americans forfeited 212 million days of earned vacation in 2017.[9] That was before the pandemic.

The problem has only worsened with the challenges of 2020, causing more managers and executives to accumulate unused vacation days. While some contracts contain the added benefit of rolling days into the next year, they are often limited to a certain number or nonexistent, depending on the individual's agreement.

But before you go packing your bags, consider that most individuals spend only 4.7% of their time per year on vacation which represents on average 17 days out of an average 262 days worked,[10] according to the U.S. Bureau of Personnel Management. That means even with vacations, we face long stretches between those three- or-four day weekends and the occasional holiday that shortens a week for us to recharge.

So what do we do? How do we get better at taking vacations that are meaningful (rest and relaxation) and memorable (reconnecting with family/friends)?

Step 1: Take control of your time off by knowing what you are entitled to. If you're not sure stop by HR and ask for a printout of your days used/available. Many companies print the information on your paystub or allow access through an employee portal connected to an absence management system.

Step 2: Plan ways to use the time by researching vacation hot spots or best vacations for your particular interests. Online travel resources and searches can put amazing vacations within reach with just a few questions to refine your search.

Step 3: Prepare a budget to ensure you get the right vacation that won't leave you stressed about paying for it. Today there are so many options that make vacationing more affordable and more enjoyable whether you are looking to go abroad or enjoy the many domestic destinations.

Step 4: Schedule the time off to ensure you actually use it. Get out the calendar and look at your workload, slower periods that afford greater opportunity to get away, or natural breaks associated with holidays.

Bottom line—we need to take the time and we need to get away! When we come back we are better, more relaxed, and more productive.

Ok, so what do we do in the meantime when vacation is still far off and we need a break now? And how do we improve our ability to recharge between vacations?

EIGHT WAYS TO RELAX WHILE WORKING

#1 LISTEN TO THE MUSIC—Not only is music enjoyable, it can help us be more productive. "Studies have shown that music produces several positive effects on a human's body and brain. Music activates both the left and right brain at the same time, and the activation of both hemispheres can maximize learning and improve memory."[11]

#2 TAKE 5—A five-minute visit if you actually go and converse with somebody about unrelated work items such as what you did last night, what you're planning on doing this weekend, something about your kids, or whatever, not only helps you get to know the people you work with, it provides that mini escape from the work that is still going to be there when you get back to your desk. Of course, if you find individuals talking more than they're working, then we have a different issue and that's a different chapter for a different book.

#3 THE MINI WALK—Try taking your lunch hour and incorporating a lei-surely walk after you've finished eating,. It doesn't have to be a workout but just gives you the ability to get outside, get some fresh air, clear your head, and take in the day. A 10- to 15-minute walk can be just a trick to help read-just and re-energize your brain for the work that's waiting.

#4 TAKE BREAKS—Breaks are not only necessary, they again give you the ability to step out from extended periods of time when you're fixated on your issues or your work. Take a 2- to 3-minute break.

#5 DECORATE—By decorating your office or workspace, you personalize your working area. By allowing your team to decorate within an approved decor, it can soften the overall appearance by transforming dull or drab work-spaces into a happy place where individuals become inspired and feel valued.

When it comes to individuals finding their happy—everybody knows what they like or don't like and again as long as it's tasteful, they should be encouraged to personalize a space. I had a secretary one time who always had flowers on her desk. I would say, "Oh, who gets the flowers?" and she would say, "I sent them to myself" or "I picked them up because I like flowers and they brighten up my desk." P-oint made.

#6 CAPITALIZE ON PD—Any time that you have an opportunity to get out of the office, away from your desk, and participate in training that allows you to improve your skillset or knowledge base—take it! This offers a break from the monotony as well as an opportunity to see others and participate in group activities.

#7 THE SEVENTH INNING STRETCH—I always thought it was cool when I went to a baseball game and they had the seventh-inning stretch. As a child I was unaware of how important it was to take that break at that point in the game. As an adult and leader I now know how important the concept is. But more importantly, the afternoon break when you've been at work for about seven hours since none of us in leadership positions work an eight- hour day. Truth be told, it's more like an average 10 to 12 hours when you factor in the time spent on work before getting to work and time spent on work after getting home.

#8 THE EIGHT O'CLOCK RULE—regardless of how much work I have at different times throughout the year I always make a point to stop working at eight o'clock and watch a movie or a show with my wife. Even if I go back to working once she goes to bed (which has happened more often than not over the past 20 years), it ensures 1) I get a break and 2) I stay married.

So does it pay to take breaks throughout the day at the expense of getting an extra 20 minutes of work in? Well that depends on the quality of those twenty minutes and more so on the quality of that work after we have maxed out our ability to focus, perform, and be sharp. We've all been there when you start drifting off mentally as others are talking to you, or you yawn as you interrupt yourself from what you are working on, kind of like losing your place and reading the same sentence multiple times.

Think about this analogy—a road trip. When you go on a road trip, the longer you drive, the harder it is to get out and walk around; if you drive too long you pass the point at which a break is helpful.

Instead if you pace yourself and drive two hours at a clip, taking a five-minute break to stretch, you can go longer and further and reach your destination more refreshed and less tired out and, trust me, your legs will work much better. Try this in a plane.

Working is the same thing. If you sit at your desk for eight hours straight, only taking minor breaks to eat and drink between hitting the keyboard, then you did not take a lunch, you did not get a break, and more importantly, you didn't take a mental break from the work you're pushing to get through. Chances are you probably are not as effective, energetic, or creative as you're capable of being with some breaks.

Now imagine a day in which you take a break after the first two and a half1/2 hours, then a lunch for a solid hour, and then come back and take another 10-minute break in the afternoon. Your productivity will amaze you, and you still have the ability to stay longer if needed. Just remember every few hours to take that 5- to 10-minute break and actually get up and change your scenery.

One thing which has served me well over the years is the ability to take a break while working. Someone may ask, "What do you mean?" What I mean is, if you put on some background music (without words), you still have the ability to punch in numbers or to read or create memos or letters and yet during those points when it doesn't require full concentration, you have the ability to enjoy the music yet focus on the work at hand.

Conversely, when you need to focus on the work element, you just forget the music and once you're past that juncture you realize, oh yeah the music is still playing. It is mindfulness practice.

Is it any different when you drive a car and listen to the radio? Other than the words to the songs, you still read the signs, gauge the traffic pattern and hopefully respect the speed limit. Then you realize that you just drove 10 miles and don't remember what you saw.

Now that we've looked at recharging to restore energy, lets focus on the need for balance in our professional as well as personal lives to ensure effectiveness as leaders.

Maintaining balance while dealing with the busy lives we have both in and out of work, dealing with family issues, social calendars, professional responsibilities, and friends is tough enough. Finding "alone time" can be even harder.

Alone time is necessary to refuel our mind and body to keep us physically and emotionally available to manage a load of personal and professional responsibilities in a beneficial way that provides the energy we need to enjoy our best time.

"Researchers suggest that being alone in nature can help people focus their priorities, gain a greater appreciation for relationships, and improve future goal-setting."[12]

Alone time allows us to reflect on what's happening, prepare mental notes to tackle our checklists, and think through strategies to deal with bigger issues. Simultaneously it can provide the escape we need to enjoy periods of pleasure, peace, and solitude that help recharge and restore our spirit, mind, and body. As leaders we need to capitalize on *alone time* to experience the benefits of both:

A 2017 study that was part of the "Solitude Project" found that those who actively choose to have alone time experience stress relief and relaxation when they spend their time alone. When we're alone, the pressures of pleasing others and social interaction are off, which can be big stressors for some people. Plus, many people choose to use their alone time to engage in relaxing activities like meditation, crafting, or yoga.[13]

For most of us, alone time comes at a real premium thanks to cell phones, email, and alerts that keep us in constant contact with the pressures of the world. We need to find ways to unplug, limit streams of information, and process tasks more effectively in and out of work to better manage our time both alone and with other people to strike the balance we need to succeed.

Quick Tips to make the most of alone time:

1. Transform drive time. Turn time spent commuting into personal enjoyment time. Sure, we all have to dodge traffic and stay alert to road conditions; however, music or books on tape can have a significant effect on our disposition by improving the ride. Time spent commuting is a golden opportunity to reflect, call friends and family (hands-free), listen to the radio, or just enjoy the scenery.

Take the Long Way Home—A classic song released in 1979 by an English progressive rock band from London14 captured our need to contemplate our lives and work through our issues while going to the place we all need to find—home.

The daily drive can also be a way to manage those needed business calls from time to time that allow you check off some of the items on your to-do list in peace and quiet without interruption other than a lane change, traffic light. or exit.

2. Manage your mood by tapping into the different genres that identify with the mood you are in to go deeper or ones that provide the lifeline to pull you out of a dark hole. Music can be "medicine" for the soul with its ability to bring happiness, understanding, or lift you when you need to be pulled out of a rut. This is why Pandora is a constant app that gets a lot of airtime on all my devices and streams through my car 80% of the time I'm alone. What makes this app so effective is the ability to customize the playlists by selecting a quick "thumbs up" or "down" to bring those selections up more often or avoid them in the future. Ultimately it allows you to fine tune your mood with favorites that won't break the conscious stream of "medicine for your soul."

3. Grab a book and take time to read or make time to read by taking your library with you on the go through Kindle, Nook, Audible, or OverDrive. Reading continues to allow us to learn, discover, escape.

4. Go DARK. Going off the grid for as little as 20 minutes can really allow us to take a break from it all—add hours, and it could be a real respite that allows us to re-engage in a way that make us more effective.

5. Wear ear buds. Listening to music as you work your way through mundane tasks can transform the task into something we look forward to and allow us to decompress, destress, and think clearer or simply experience enjoyment. When you still need to hear others or answer calls, pull out the buds and turn down the music to where it does not interfere with others and allows you to do what is necessary to accomplish your work.

The challenge that exists in finding balance is centered around the concept and dilemma of what constitutes the right degree of balance. What is the perfect balance for managing our lives? Is it a 50/50 proposition? Or should it be evenly dissected or compartmentalized by the various aspects of our lives with the major focus on career and family or a weighted value that is career-heavy?

The answer is just as unique as each situation and individual but it is firmly rooted in the connection between happiness and purpose.

Therefore, we need to find the balance that works for us and satisfies the demands that are emergent while keeping those that are pressing from overtaking us. That is why organization is vital to managing, performing, and accomplishing tasks.

A good friend and fellow speaker, Dan Thurmon, seized on this concept in his book, *Off Balance on Purpose,* which identifies the struggle of finding "balance" in our lives. He captures the feelings of frustration and inadequacy as we become overwhelmed trying to obtain a perfect balance that does not exist—at least not in a perfect framework of an equal distribution between everything that pulls at us. "The perpetual quest for balance ends up limiting growth, progress, and the quality of life."[15]

Dan's book was originally published in 2009, yet the challenge of finding balance has only intensified as the demands on us as leaders continue to grow, especially with the added challenges of COVID-19.

In an upcoming *Lunch & Learn* series to be presented by our state association of school business administrators (NJASBO), the topic set to air via Zoom from an affiliate group (Illinois ASBO) titled, "Work-Life -Balance: The Difference Between Success and Burnout," demonstrates the broad appeal and concern for dealing with the struggle.

So here we are a decade later, still trying to find ways to achieve greater balance with the intent of reducing overall stress.

Part of being organized is knowing when to take certain actions and, conversely, when to stop or take a breather.

Here are seven tips to improve our ability to organize and accomplish our workloads:

1. Know when to take a break—pushing through at the cost of exhaustion and getting muscle aches not only wears us out, it compromises the accuracy and quality of the work. Remember a break can be short and therefore allow us to go longer and stay stronger.
2. Know when to move on (abort)—When the breaks aren't doing it and we start taking too many or extending the time spent relaxing, it's probably time to leave. Putting some distance between you and project you're working on allows for the body and mind to be refreshed and hit the ground running the next day.
3. Know when to ask for help—Why struggle and prolong the agony? When we work with great teams, it means they operate with trust—that means you can always ask for help, assistance, or simply a quick review to validate our concern(s) or reinforce our progress.
4. Know when to give it up—Some things will never work and learning from failed attempts is helpful; however, continuing to fail without changing our inputs is insanity and can become disastrous. Knowing when to give up in this case is really knowing when to move on.

5. Know when to dig in—This is just the opposite as we see the light at the end of the tunnel and simply need to buckle down and do the work. While the concept is easy to understand, leaders who struggle with this are often those who *under-delegate* and put too much work on themselves.

6. Know when to clear the mind—Clearing our mind can be an instant break that does not require formal movement away from the task at hand. It just means take a momentary "Zen" break to mentally refocus on what you are processing, building, developing, or solving.

   For situations requiring more extensive mind relaxation perhaps consider introducing meditation as regular practice into your daily life to improve mental health and bring about positive changes in your mood.

7. Know when to use the team—Some projects are just too big to manage alone, and others, while they can be individual projects, would benefit from the strength of the team by working collaboratively. This allows for creativity as well as shorter duration for completion times.

Chapter 8

Avoiding Burnout

In 1979, legendary Canadian-American singer Neil Young was singing about another place that we should avoid, *fading away*; he called it going "into the black." "Hey Hey, My My" was written by Young in collaboration with the punk rock band DEVO, and the words to the song became part of a different kind of anthem that caught on, spending five weeks in the Top 100 on Billboard and peaking at 79 on November 3, 1979.[1] But unlike the Staple Singers' anthem, promising to take us where we want to go, Young's song warns us that we don't want to lose importance or slowly disappear; therefore, "It's better to burn out than fade away!"[2]

But truth be told, the lines that follow capture the reality of the situation dealing with *burnout* and that is, "Once you're gone, you can't come back,"[3]—falling out of the "blue" and into the "black."[4]

SO HOW DO WE STAY IN THE PINK?

Trying to stay upbeat and stress-free today is harder than ever. Instead, we tend to find ourselves playing "beat the clock" by struggling to keep up on all the things we are responsible for managing. Trying to keep up with our responsibilities (work, those we are responsible for, career, family, and friends) is nearly impossible, as something always seems to give. More often than not we find ourselves re-prioritizing, shifting energy, and sacrificing either family -over -work or work -over -family and eventually burning the candle at both ends, or simply burning out.

That's why we need a break—that's why we need a vacation—time to get away, and time to unwind.

But the reality is, this is not always possible nor practical depending on what is happening at the time. Stress tends to increase during periods of difficulty, high work volume, and deadlines which at the same time require our constant presence, attention, and focus.

Tax accountants for instance do not enjoy spring break; however, that's exactly when they could use one. "Tax specialists often work long hours during the tax season"—an understatement, say accountants. "In fact, the period leading up to April 15—the source of both income and exhaustion—is the "Christmas shopping" season for many accountants."[5]

In 2018 the World Health Organization (WHO) recognized *burnout* as global phenomenon that was spreading throughout the workplace and, as such, included it in their International Classification of Diseases 11th Revision (ICD-11)—the global standard for diagnostic health information.

Burnout is a syndrome conceptualized as resulting from chronic workplace stress that has not been successfully managed. It is characterized by three dimensions: 1) feelings of energy depletion or exhaustion; 2) increased mental distance from one's job, or feelings of negativism or cynicism related to one's job; and 3) a sense of ineffectiveness and lack of accomplishment. Burnout refers specifically to phenomena in the occupational context and should not be applied to describe experiences in other areas of life.[6]

So again the question before us remains—How do we avoid burnout and remain physically and emotionally at our best, when time to ourselves is limited and demands on our time remain boundless? Answer: We need to manage to fit breaks into our schedule and add moments of happiness, pleasure, and enjoyment into our daily routines.

The answer has LEADERSHIP written all over it. With millions of health books and a plethora of "How-To" books on the market, it basically comes down to this simple LEADERSHIP formula of *4 less, 4 more, and 2 better*:

1. Less screen time—Problems stemming from too much screen time are often associated with adolescents who consume too much TV, play video games for hours on end, and engage in heavy cell phone usage. While research-based articles link excessive screen time to anxiety and mood disorders among this segment, we need to recognize the same

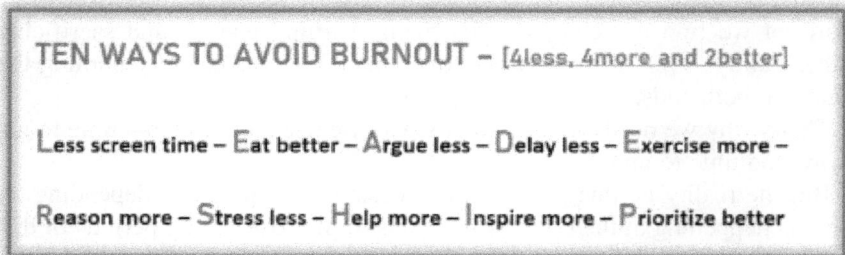

TEN WAYS TO AVOID BURNOUT – [4less, 4more and 2better]

Less screen time – Eat better – Argue less – Delay less – Exercise more –

Reason more – Stress less – Help more – Inspire more – Prioritize better

Figure 8.1. Ten Ways to Avoid Burnout.

concerns are present with adults who spend too much time on devices or in front of computers.

"Today's adults have been estimated to spend more than 10 hours a day in front of screens (Harvard T. H. Chan School of Public Health). Because the activity is sedentary, this exposure has been linked, in part, to higher obesity rates (which can lead to diabetes) and sleep problems."[7]

"Additionally, when asked, 15 percent of adults reported that they were more likely to lose focus at work due to checking their cellphone, which is double the number of teens who have trouble focusing in class for that same reason."[8]

None of us are immune to the tendency of forming bad habits, and increasing our screen time through a justification of being work-related is no exception. This is one sure way of heading down the wrong path that leads to burnout. Take Arianna Huffington, syndicated columnist, co-founder of *The Huffington Post*, the founder and CEO of Thrive Global, and noted author.

During a May 2019 podcast interview, she opened up about her collapse from burnout and exhaustion two years into building *Huffington*.[9] In her words, "We had so much data and science about how [chronic stress] was affecting performance, productivity, and business metrics like attrition, retention, and healthcare costs." Arianna notes that despite our world being so data-driven, she and others were "ignoring the data and continuing to live under the delusion that in order to succeed you have to burn out. That somehow burnout was the price of success."

Placing cell phones or devices off for periods of time each day or out of reach when trying to relax is a good way to limit the constant checking on unimportant notifications. Turning off notifications from many apps is an even better way to preserve your time and manage it better by doing what you need to do or focusing on what really matters. Checking email throughout the day at intervals is more productive and allows us to focus on bigger projects or tasks that need our attention. Likewise, we become better listeners when speaking with others, as our attention is not on the device but on the individual and therefore we not distracted.

2. Eat better—Eating better has so many benefits related to health, energy, mood, and appearance that it stands to reason we should all be doing it; however, for various reasons including our busy schedules we skip meals, starve our bodies of the nutrients they need, and pack on the calories to overcompensate.

That just about describes anyone feeling the pressure and stress of needing to get things done and not finding enough hours in the day— sound familiar? "Poor nutrition doesn't just impact our health, it can affect our performance at work by negatively impacting concentration and energy levels, and cause irritability, frustration and impatience."[10] The Aetna article focuses on seven key strategies to ensuring healthy eating at work that center on educating yourself to make simple and better choices, incorporating thought into planning your meals by developing a routine, avoid skipping meals, staying hydrated, smart lunching, sensible snacking, and mindful eating. Again, *whenever we focus on something we get better at it*; meal planning and healthier choices in what we eat are no exception.

3. Argue less—It has long been known that arguments produce negative effects on the body including raised blood pressure. A University of California, Irvine study showed, "Chronic stress is considered an important factor in elevation of blood pressure, which is considered a major cause of heart disease."[11] Scientists in Germany at the Max Planck Institute for Cognitive and Brain Sciences in Leipzig and the Technische Universität in Dresden concluded that just observing another person in a stressful situation such as an argument can cause the release of cortisol, a stress hormone, in their own bodies.[12] Their findings revealed a direct correlation between stress and burnout linked to contact with stressed individuals:

> Stress is a major health threat in today's society. It causes a range of psychological problems like burnout, depression and anxiety. Even those who lead relatively relaxed lives constantly come into contact with stressed individuals. Whether at work or on television: someone is always experiencing stress, and this stress can affect the general environment in a physiologically quantifiable way through increased concentrations of the stress hormone cortisol.[13]

So based on the findings—not only should we refrain from unwelcomed stress due to arguments in and out of the workplace, we should make every effort as leaders to promote stress-free environments and take action to mitigate stressful situations and avoid or end arguments when they happen.

With respect to improving workplace environments to mitigate stress, implementation of wellness plans and policies are a good place to start. Work with your human resources department along with reaching out to health insurance providers.

4. Delay less—Get a jump on stress by getting the things done that need doing! A simple yet effective concept, because we feel better and more in control when things are done or in progress as they move closer to completion. This is how we shrink the list of what's left and begin to

feel the weight come off that can be crushing as more and more tasks begin to pile up.

Let's talk about multi-tasking. Multi-tasking is one of the most overused and misunderstood terms in place today by those that want to convey a sense of operational efficiency by giving off the impression of Superman or Wonder Woman at work.

Multi-tasking in its truest form is not doing ten things at once; that is not what we need, nor is it what you want to see. The reality is that quality and focus goes down as each additional task is added. In truth, we need to do more than one thing at a time; however, we need to retain the same attention to detail and focus on ensuring quality work is being produced by devoting our full *time and attention* to each aspect of the task at hand in order to avoid mistakes, malfunctions, and bigger problems down the road.

Therefore, we need to multi-task in a way that allows us to "park a project" at some stage while we either finish another or simply complete elements of multiple projects while we wait for others, information, or materials. Understanding this and, more importantly, creating the ability to do this without compromising the integrity of our projects or making mistakes when we come back to where we left off depends on an individual's ability to maintain attention to detail and accurately mark where they left off to keep their place. Keep in mind: working on multiple projects or completing various parts of tasks in segments is not the same a multi-tasking as we are not doing them all at the same time; we are simply jumping from one project or task to another and thus completing various assignments throughout the day.

Project delays can also be costly as the price of goods and services escalate over time and during shortages, or material and labor costs can escalate at a much faster rate month over month. "When a project is delayed, financing costs rise and the project doesn't generate the planned revenue. Sometimes you can mitigate these effects, because, while part of the project may be delayed, other parts might be ready for service and revenue generation."[14] So don't delay . . . get going.

5. Exercise more—Most people associate exercise with grueling workouts that requires equipment, a gym membership, and time to commit to a rigid plan. This is great if you are single and have the time and discipline, but what if you are juggling a career and family? What if you simply aren't that person that can commit to a regular routine that incorporates a vigorous workout?

While working out reduces stress, we can get caught up in the stress of not working out and, given enough pressure and anxiety, the effects can be worse than missing the cardio or Pilates that we had planned on doing.

Exercising more is simply about getting up and getting active. Do what you enjoy but move more—walking, running, dancing, stretching—through hiking, golfing, tennis, aerobics, bowling, it really doesn't matter. Low-intensity workouts are better than sitting and snacking, and they help reduce stress.

By setting realistic goals that are obtainable and fun, we can protect against quitting quickly or falling off our routines by skipping days that turn into weeks until we have abandoned our plans altogether.

"The most common reason people give for not exercising is that they simply do not have the time for it. Whether it is due to work, family, children, or a combination of these, you may say that exercise just does not fit into your busy schedule."[15]

Try simple strategies like walking more often when possible, parking further from the entrance of stores or buildings, taking the stairs, or simply riding a bike. Lawn work or cleaning can also count as a way to get blood flowing and muscles moving in addition to any exercise you may incorporate into your weekly routine. According to the Mayo Clinic, individuals should "Aim for at least 30 minutes of moderate physical activity every day. If you want to lose weight, maintain weight loss or meet specific fitness goals, you may need to exercise more."[16]

6. Reason more—Think things through and find better solutions to your problems based on logic and reality. Reason stems from the Latin ration- or ratio, "reckoning, calculation, explanation,"[17] and as such, allows us to think logically and therefore gain a better understanding of the situations we face. It equips us with the ability to solve and it improves our judgement in ascertaining what must be done. Often the solutions are apparent once we focus on the issue at hand, whether it is problem solving, decision making, or simply prioritizing the tasks we are given to achieve resolution and thus reduce our stress levels.

   Once we find ourselves engaged in addressing issues, we are far less stressed than dwelling over what the issue(s) are because we have now put our thoughts into action and doing something, which in this case is better than doing nothing. However, applying reason improves our outcomes as they are now grounded in reality and include justification for those actions.

7. Stress less—Stress is a killer and it can become an obsession. Some people stress about everything, and it becomes a pattern or behavior that plagues their daily lives. As leaders we need to steer clear of the negativity, fear, and worry that promotes stress in our workplace, our

ability to manage our critical tasks, and our responsibilities regarding supervision.

The reality is, stress does exist and we certainly cannot avoid it; however, we can learn to manage it and keep it from overtaking us. Start by "going positive" and avoiding negativity! Every time we are confronted with a situation or individual and we are not exactly sure of the outcome or situation that presents itself, go positive and assume the best instead of the worst. Regardless of the situation—your ability to cope or deal with that situation will improve as your stress levels go down. There is a ton of research out there that supports this fact, but you need to own it, adopt it, and implement it as part of your routine.

8. Help more—Helping others is therapeutic and it takes us into positive territory. This can be accomplished at work or on our own time through organizations that promote opportunities to help.

We feel good when we help others, so let's focus on doing it more. However, some people can do too much volunteering and helping and again become overwhelmed, overcommitted, and worn out, thus back on the stress train—so be careful.

9. Inspire more—By inspiring others, we achieve a level of personal satisfaction as leaders that is simply not available absent this pursuit. When we inspire we move from simply being in charge to being dynamic by influencing positive outcomes for others who take our lessons, advice, and direction and put these into practical application in their own settings. That is what leadership is all about and what makes us not only feel good, but validated in our efforts and work—the payoff!

Indeed.com, the #1 job site in the world with over 250 million unique visitors every month, published an article in December 2020 under their career development tab titled "How to Practice Inspirational Leadership." The article discusses the qualities of an inspirational leader and the importance of modeling them for your teams. "The best leaders aim to inspire their team toward personal and professional success and create a culture of motivation in their workplace."[18]

The article points out the benefits of inspiration leadership that include meeting goals, increasing engagement, and creating committed employees; however, the important benefit to the leader is the improved operations along with goal attainment which reduces stress as we rack up another win in the win column.

Again, *simple but powerful* as the rules of reciprocity exist in the exchange, producing a *win-win* atmosphere and less stress for all involved, as accomplishment and goal attainment equate to a better sense of health and well-being centered around fulfillment and achievement.

10. Prioritize better—When it comes to task prioritization, we simply need to consider the importance assigned to each task based on immediacy, available resources, and staff.

Task prioritization and development of an *attack plan* can help you improve your time management by considering which task(s) need to be accomplished "right -now" versus what can "wait." In addition to evaluating prioritization based on importance and time sensitivity, we need to consider "knocking -off" tasks that are quick and easy to accomplish in order to shrink the list, gain a sense of progress, and improve focus on the larger tasks.

Additionally, some tasks require assistance, coordination with others, or teaming in order to reach successful resolution. This provides an understanding of the complexity of the task(s) and begins the mapping process to determine resources needed, completion time, scheduling requirements, and allocation of those resources and a general timeline of milestones. Again, depending on the magnitude of the project, it may require tools such as a Gantt chart to effectively manage and track the progress. In these instances, you need to realize that it's not going to be done quickly and you will have down time throughout the project to focus on other tasks that can be completed—thus checking off other items from your list.

While these ten strategies are designed to help us as leaders from experiencing burnout, we need to think about our stars (high performers) to protect them from burnout as well.

Consider the relevance of actual stars to the concept. Stars are measured in magnitude and luminosity based on their distance from the earth and brightness (how bright they appear). While science outlines the process of going dwarf (dying), which takes millions or billions of years depending on size and mass of the star, the observable fact is the brighter stars shine, the quicker they burn out as they are "visible to the naked eye in this stage of their life cycles."[19] Now reflect on our stars who exhibit accelerated performance and achievement, thus earning them the title of "rock star": they shine brighter than their counterparts, and we appreciate having them. We need them in our organizations to achieve our goals and outperform expectations. While we enjoy such performance and continue to benefit from their enthusiasm, motivation, and self-reliance, we need to guard against burnout by ensuring they are recharging along the way and resting up in -between successes.

This goes with the problems associated with thinking you are indispensable, that no one can pick up the slack if you're out, and things are only done right if you are there to do them. That's a problem, and one that plagues most newly minted leaders who feel they have to control every situation by being personally involved and dealing with every single issue. Not only is it harmful, it's not practical.

At the same time, we have a golden opportunity to develop staff or junior leaders who are waiting for the opportunity to step up and take over in our absence, to prove they have what it takes to lead in their own right. This is why we have them, and this is how continuity of leadership works. Insecure leaders see this as a threat; however, great leaders expect this and plan for this in order to truly enjoy their time away.

It takes some managers years to realize their organizations and, more importantly, their teams can manage during short absences such as vacation. Well-trained teams provide necessary coverage and most "emergencies" are nothing that can't be handled or dealt with until the manager returns. High-level issues typically allow for other managers to step in and cover, which in turn provides stronger team coverage for all managers. Today there are always ways to connect if necessary, in the event of a critical need; however, vacations remain a critical need of their own for managers to recharge and return ready for the next set of challenges.

Don't waste part of your vacation constantly checking in on what is going on—if something comes up the team can handle it, and if there is a true emergency, they will reach out to you. This is your time to be with family and friends. If not, you will find yourself just beginning to relax by the time the vacation is about to end. Vacations are made to enjoy and relax—so enjoy them and use the time to reconnect with those close to you or just time away to clear your mind and find peace.

Peace empowers us to see clearly in the midst of every challenge. Our greatest challenge is finding it.

Chapter 9

Staying Organized and Focused (the Hammer, the Rock, and the In-Box)

Keeping pace with the high volume of traffic that comes across our desks, the meetings that fill our calendars, and the mail/emails that fill our in-boxes is about staying organized, and staying organized is about learning how to manage, juggle, and address information and issues in today's busy world.

We are all familiar with wisdom quotes related to "life" described as more a journey than a race for good reason: to ensure we are wise enough to control our energy, momentum, and pace to govern our speed, manage our effort, and finish each race. In doing so, we become pacesetters for ourselves.

In the world of long-distance running, pacesetters are runners who "lead middle- or long-distance running events for the first section to ensure a fast time and avoid excessive tactical racing."[1] They serve to keep runners from going too fast or too slow by gauging the speed needed to maintain their goal of not only finishing the race but posting their "best time." Their actions benefit the field as they are setting the pace for runners, allowing them to find their rhythm and ensure they have enough in the tank for the big finish.

In the same way pacesetters help the field to control their effort and use/ conserve the right amount of energy to go the distance, we need to apply the same strategy in our careers to ensure they are not short-lived but instead full with longevity, accomplishment, and meaning—that is how legacies are built. That is what sets great leaders apart from ordinary leaders.

Staying organized allows us to keep pace with the busy schedules we juggle, the information we process, and the records we maintain that become important in recording the resolution to issues we face and the tasks we have completed.

Keeping pace or keeping up with all our demands requires the same mastery of personal energy that a runner employs to win their race. Depending on the urgency and severity of our situation(s), our races are not all the same in duration—some are quick sprints and others, long-distance marathons.

At the same time, jugging our schedules and commitments is about finding balance to meet all our obligations in a way that keeps us fresh, responsive, and effective—versus worn-out, unapproachable, and unproductive.

The key to organization is knowing what's important and then knowing how to manage work by keeping track of it as you address it in order to resolve or dispose of it.

Being organized at work allows more time for balance in other aspects of our lives, and that comes from employing systems and processes that allow us to cut through the work in the shortest amount of time without compromising the quality of the work.

Having systems in place for handling materials, information, data, and correspondence helps improve our effectiveness at managing our responsibilities, from urgent matters to daily tasks as well as projects. By being organized, we ensure a process exists to avoid chaos or haphazard searches that would find us scrambling to respond to a deadline that is now looming or already expired. That puts unnecessary stress on us and undue stress on our teams.

Case in point—the disorganized leader: There was a superintendent who was brilliant at managing situations and people. He had a knack for reading the room and was well versed in matters of curriculum, instruction, and process and organizational management; however, he had one major weakness—organization. His office was referred to as "the abyss." Whatever went into that office found its way into unmarked files, boxes, or piles that cluttered his desk, a spare desk, his conference table, chairs, counters, and even the floor.

To make matter worse, whenever he had a meeting involving board members or district administrators, he would do the quick cleanup by grabbing stacks and putting them into file boxes, akin to a kid cleaning their room by dumping everything in the closet.

Whatever paper went into that office rarely came out without hours of searching through stacks of reports, boxes of correspondence, and reams of paper. The worst part was he had no idea himself where things were, and from time to time a team of secretaries would search through mountains of information only to find other reports, studies, or correspondence that were no longer necessary, or previous versions of a final product without notations as to which version was the latest or fact-checked. Therefore, it was easier in most cases to just start over and end up repeating work that had already been done.

So how did he function? How did the office function? The answer is—slowly!

The district was a top performer and others around him, including his staff and district administrators, made up for the weakness by compensating for his lack of organization. They kept copies of correspondence, proposals, memos, or whatever they shared with him when possible to avoid the fire drill that became a scene of great confusion and quite messy. It was actually funny at times because he was so likable—he would laugh like a kid being scolded for not cleaning their room—but it was a time killer and, as a result, reports were filed late, meetings were delayed or went longer than necessary, or we just ended up doing things twice.

This is NOT how we should work, nor is it productive in managing our time and the time of staff members. Being disorganized as a leader is harmful to everyone involved and places unnecessary strain on the balance we all strive to achieve.

So how do we get organized? Start by prioritizing the work and keeping track of it as we process it. So what do you do with files that are in -process? They exist but need to be within reach as you work with them over shorter and longer periods of time; however, they are active and not ready to reside in the filing cabinet.

Answer: Come up with a system or organization that works for you in your situation, based on what you manage. "Surveys show the average person loses an hour a day to disorganization."[2] We need to create work space that works—starting with our desk. "In the office, your desk is your command center. And experts said how well it's organized can help set the tone and productivity level at work."[3]

Managing your command center (the desk) starts by organizing what's on it and arranging it according to your system. Ultimately it is your desk and you need to make it work; however, you want to ensure it is not adding to your stress or drawing the wrong type of attention. Most important is the assignment of a priority scale by levels. This will immediately sort items into classifications such as: Urgent and Important; Urgent but Less Important; Important -but -Not -Urgent; and Neither Important -nor -Urgent.

My own system revolves around four key components for personal organization that classify all items that cross my desk: -the Rock (long-term projects), the Hammer (short-term projects), the in-box (sorter bin), plus the wastebasket (round file). They start with the in-box and travel through to completion and filing in either the round file (wastebasket) or permanent file (file bank).

THE ROCK—The rock sits atop files containing projects required to be completed, or innovative ideas representing future plans to be advanced, and sometimes simply concepts that I would like to explore, but are not pressing (Important -but -Not -Urgent). Whenever there is down time, which seems to be less and less these days, or in the case of projects that become time sensitive, I pull the ones that need attention or the ones I simply wish to advance. Sometimes I work on them to a point and then return them to their place under the rock.

Once they advance to a point of completion or priority, they move to either the hammer (working) or the file bank.

THE HAMMER—Is a paperweight that sits atop other files that are "active" and therefore constantly in play (Urgent and Important, as well as items that are Urgent but less Important). It serves as a daily reminderof work that needs to be done, and these files contain time-sensitive materials that need to be acted on.

By design they are closer to the phone and computer, allowing easy access throughout the day to prep for meetings, and retrieval of information while working or waiting to be processed, then tossed or filed based on need.

THE IN-BOX—Now more than ever, the traditional inbox remains important to processing information, including moving it laterally to a place under the rock or hammer, or allowing that information to get routine attention in the form of signatures and immediate processing to return to other in-boxes or simply reviewed and filed in the file bank or the round file (the garbage can).

The takeaway is to make your own system of organization by finding out what works best for you to get organized and stay organized, and ultimately setting a pace for addressing and completing the tasks that need to be done, leaving you with time to spare for other commitments or activities.

Moving on to filing—filing is a key component to any organizational plan in any office, but it goes beyond the filing cabinet or archiving records. It starts with building and processing files, even electronic files, with a system that is searchable.

TIPS ON HOW TO IMPROVE FILING

1. Color—Color-coded files allow you to file according to subject while you are working with files for easy identification by groups. An example would be using green files for revenue or budgetary information, red for facilities or work orders, blue for administrative matters, and yellow for policy or memos. The actual color assignment or symbolism is purely up to the user; however, working with multiple files until they are ready to move to a permanent file bank can keep them at your fingertips, and colors make it faster and easier to locate the information you need.

2. Labeling—Want to lose something fast? Put it in a manila folder without a label. After a while you have a slew of folders that all look alike. Now you are forced to go through each folder in search of the one you want. Worse yet is when someone picked up the file and put it down

somewhere else. In larger offices this can result in files "going miss-ing," even though they never left the building.

Even if you mark it temporarily in pencil until you get a typed label, you avoid the possibility of losing track of the folder's contents or where the folder should reside.

3. Grouping—By grouping files into categories, we create a *one-stop shopping* opportunity for ourselves and others to peruse, search, and find important information when it is needed. Regardless of whether we are looking at "paper" or electronic filing, organization is what saves time and eliminates headaches, aggravation and, ultimately, increases productivity.

4. Labeling System—Develop a system and stick with it. Provide training on the filing method adopted for your office (alphabetical by subject or name, etc.), and prepare a legend. Be sure to keep the legend handy so it serves as a key to avoid unnecessary searching which wastes time and adds stress.

   When files are kept without a system, we can lose important docu-ments that remain under our roof. Notes or memory aids help by trigger-ing information that is helpful in maintaining a trail to provide quicker access to files and can be inserted into files with multiple uses or implications: An audit note, for instance, may be in a purchasing file to document efforts taken for compliance with purchasing laws related to a specific bid. If you look into the bid folder, the same note can redirect you to the purchase order or simply note the information in the file for cross referencing.

   Whatever system and method you agree upon, be consistent and stay with it. Ensure all files are labeled the same way, in the same position, and filed according to the universal system for the master files to pre-vent chaos.

5. Purging—Getting rid of inactive files that are no longer required to be kept by the organization allows room for new files and room in general as the number of filing cabinets goes down. This requires a records retention schedule that lists the minimum legal and fiscal time periods that records must be retained. Depending on the type of business you are in, you should be following either IRS rules or state and local gov-ernmental regulations.

   Retention periods are determined in conformance with state and fed-eral codes, regulations, and statutes of limitation.

   Annual purging of files allows for the filing system to stay vital, as required information is current and necessary information is either still on file or archived. An added step to ensure those files are properly destroyed is simply scheduling an approved on-site shredding company with immediate or witnessed destruction of confidential, copyrighted, or royalty-based materials directly on premises.

6. Date Stamp with Time for the Latest Version—This is extremely important when organizations are *under the gun* to produce records, find invoices, or pull files related to audits, inspections, request for documents, or simply updating reports that rely on previous reports. The easiest way to know you have the latest draft or final document is to see the date/time stamp on the bottom of the file.

Oftentimes individuals or departments receive audit recommendations when they fail to document the proper records or provide documentation to answer queries or support the actions that were taken or, better yet, those that were required to be compliant with applicable rules or regulations. In this case the group ends up receiving the recommendation not because they did it wrong, but because they cannot prove they did it right.

Returning to prioritization, the U.S. Army Signal Corps developed proven techniques and practices for handling message traffic in secured telecommunications stations throughout the world. They prioritize message traffic, stamping it IMMEDIATE, ROUTINE, IMPORTANT, URGENT; or FLASH, then process it through a series of logs, notations, and proper handling procedures. According to the stamp, certain information is elevated above other information.

Now think about your organization and your structure for receiving and processing information. What are you handling each day that is considered critical information? What cannot wait and needs "eyes on" immediately? To properly and effectively prioritize information, consider these critical elements of information processing:

a. Time Management
b. Task Prioritization
c. Assigning Value
d. Assigning Importance
e. Stamping or Branding the Information

With proper handling of sensitive documents and consistent practices for daily correspondence (written/electronic), along with filing systems that accurately preserve and allow for easy recall of information, documents and data can operate more efficiently and therefore more effectively. Thus, staying organized becomes part of our daily routines rather than extra work or an unwelcomed project.

PART IV

Voyagers

Chapter 10

Speaking Out

Sharing Our Wisdom and Expertise

One critical pathway available to all leaders as they journey to success lies in taking advantage of professional speaking opportunities. Whether you intend to speak professionally or wish to improve your speaking skills to become more comfortable addressing large groups—public speaking allows leaders to share their message, expertise, and wisdom.

When we broaden our leadership to include engaging audiences outside of our departments, companies, or organizations, we seize opportunities to connect. When that connection inspires others, we grow our leadership through influence, networking, and teaching. Putting ourselves out there to share our wealth of knowledge allows us to stay sharp by staying current with trends, research, and application. But it carries an added benefit of interactive dialog with groups and individuals who add to the mix of excitement, enthusiasm, and knowledge of our subject matter.

Speaking gets you noticed, and depending on what leg of the leadership journey you are on, it can propel you forward ahead of your peers. That is providing you are ready for the opportunity and prepared to make the most of it. When inexperienced leaders jump too quickly or dive headfirst into presentations they are not yet prepared for, they risk getting negative attention. That can happen for several reasons, including lack of preparation, lack of experience, limited depth of knowledge, and poor communication skills.

To guard against these issues that can wreck a presentation or push us off course, let's consider them further and look at prevention tips that can help us navigate around them. The prevention tips are designed to help avoid bad performances, improve poor performances, and manage good presentations.

ELEMENTS OF BAD PRESENTATIONS
AND HOW TO AVOID THEM

- **Lack of Preparation**—When we prepare, it shows and when we do not. . . it is obvious. Meaningful presentations are ones that people remember, leave with valuable takeaways, and apply from notes, comments or advice by putting them into practice. This allows for professional growth and marks the presenter as a master teacher.

  - *Prevention Tips:*

    1. Prepare for potential questions and have the answers available and at the ready. Better yet, develop a Q&A and put it into the presentation. Review your material for any weakness and shore up points that are vague, bland, convoluted, or overcomplicated.
    2. Rehearse the presentation and get others to review it and provide feedback—make sure they are trusted to give you honest feedback to overcome and improve mediocre presentations. Focus groups are easy to form, and individuals appreciate being chosen or selected for something important.
    3. Arrive early and check the equipment to ensure everything is working properly before you start. Once it's "go -time," you do not want to make things awkward by realizing people cannot hear you or your slides are not working. While all speakers need to contend with technical issues that arise at the most inopportune times, those who complete pre-checks are less likely to get flustered when it happens than those who skip this step because they know it was tested and working prior to their start.
- **Lack of Experience**—When inexperienced leaders address large peer groups, they tend to underestimate the wealth of experience in the room, leaving them vulnerable to sharpshooters who question the information presented. When this happens, the speaker needs to be prepared to respond in a cogent manner or risk losing the room and watching the presentation crash and burn.

  - *Prevention Tips:*

    1. Partner up with an experienced colleague that has presentation experience in addition to experience with the subject matter. Co-presenting allows less-experienced speakers to gain valuable experience in public speaking with a safety net, allowing the more experienced speaker to step in and take the challenging questions or expand on more difficult responses.

2. Try interviewing specialists or experts in the field who may not be available for the presentation but may be accessible in preparation for needed quotes, adding legitimacy to the information.

3. Consider video conferencing to add experts as panelists. Given the recent familiarization with Zoom and other video conferencing tools, as a result of COVID closures, consider allowing for experts to join into presentations seamlessly via video conferencing as needed.

• **Limited Depth of Knowledge**—Cursory or limited knowledge can lead to insufficient or inadequate presentations that lack importance in both meaning and usefulness. Professional development that lacks either of these two components results in poor attendance, audiences that are unengaged, or even walkouts. Worse yet, it damages the professional reputation of the speaker as they are seen for what they are—limited. Keep in mind the network effect,- as now you become a known commodity but not for what you seek.

If nothing else, future speaking opportunities become scarce and limited as those "in the know" know not to consider you, thus allowing others to move ahead in this sector of leadership.

Limited *depth of knowledge*, in part, results from a *lack of experience* since information and skills are both acquired through experience and education; however, without experience, one cannot acquire holistic knowledge, only theoretical or book knowledge. Lacking practical hands-on experience poses limitations on the depth of knowledge which puts the speaker at risk regarding credibility.

• *Prevention Tips:*

1. Put time into researching your topic by gathering applicable facts, figures, and statistics if available. Use simple charts, graphs, and infographics that tell your story or convey the information in an easy-to-digest format. Build or use graphics that allow an individual to consume the message and commit it to memory in seconds.

2. Build knowledge through reading, participating in webinars and workshops, and watching videos designed to impart knowledge specific to certain subject matter. Just keep in mind you need to ensure a full understanding of the subject matter forward and backward prior to presenting that topic to others, especially on a large stage.

3. Take advantage of online courses and discussion groups to expand your knowledge and glean additional knowledge from others.

    "Building your knowledge base is a long-term process that expands through life. But it isn't a linear mechanism. Instead, it follows an exponential rise . . . because of the connections that your intellect is able to make between newly gained insight and existing knowledge."[1]

- **Poor Communication Skills**—Poor communication skills can kill a presentation even if the presenter has vast knowledge and plenty of experience with the subject matter. Engaging presentations require engaging speakers to deliver the content by grabbing and keeping the audience's attention. In today's digital environment with personal devices and ISP access to the internet, you can lose an audience quickly once you lose eye contact.

  Mastering communication skills means understanding the basics of getting your message or point across to compel the listener or audience to focus and retain the information presented.

- *Prevention Tips:*

  1. Maintain focus on you as the presenter and not on your slides or other medium by limiting the number of slides in the deck, reducing the amount of content per slide (death-by-PowerPoint) and limiting the amount of animation to find that perfect synergy between your message, the material shared, and audience engagement.
  2. Allow for spontaneous conversation and questions when looking to add energy into the presentation when it fits or when you need to turn up audience engagement, but make sure you continue to control the pace, the topic, and especially the room. Don't let it get away from you and become a distraction.
  3. Be engaging by using stories to support your points, avoid monotone speaking by using proper inflection, enunciation, and emphasis where appropriate. Avoid overemphasizing every point or a sing-song cadence and lastly, pause for effect to allow key points to sink in.

     When speakers are flat, they come across as lacking personality and are considered boring. Again, you do not want to lose an audience; getting their attention back is hard because they have already determined they are not interested in what you have to say. The beginning is your opportunity to grab them and once you have them "hooked"—never let them go.

So now you are ready to engage any audience on any topic, right?—wrong. First, you must consider a few more variables when charting your course to presenting, speaking, or teaching by considering three key elements of presenting: the *venue*, the *event*, and the *audience*.

1. The Venue—Size matters; you need to match your presentation to the stage, whether that stage is a small conference room or a large event center. Begin by *measuring your message*—based on the size of the

venue, -you will need to size that message to fit accordingly. Typically, professional event space ranges from 50 to 300 seating capacity, allowing a speaker to work the room while delivering their presentation in an up-close and personal setting. However, larger venues such as a performing arts center could range from 1,000 to 3,000 seats, requiring a stage presence and larger message and necessitating a stage production to include sound and lighting.

Knowing the venue and getting comfortable with it is critical to delivering a powerful presentation. "How is the room arranged? Is it auditorium seating or classroom seating? Are there enough seats for the expected number of attendees? Will you be on stage or on the floor? It is important to note the arrangement of the room so you can be prepared to address your audience in the most engaging way. Will you be able to walk around the room? Will you be speaking from a podium? You want to get a feel for the layout so you know what to expect on the day of your presentation."[2]

2. The Event—Determines the audience and the venue and therefore aids in helping you research and prepare ahead of time. Depending on the event, you can already gain an understanding of parameters for your message—how formal it should be and your degree of interaction with the group. It also impacts the degree of exposure, be it local, regional, state, or national, again helping to determine the appropriate level based on your experience with speaking. If you haven't given a presentation before, you might want to try presenting at the county or regional level before tackling a state or national event, especially if you're going solo. A good rule of thumb is to wait until you have at least five years of experience (real experience) prior to applying to present at a state or national conference.

3. The Audience—Knowing your audience is the key to making a connection. It starts by ensuring you understand who they are: professional makeup, age range, education level, and what their struggles or needs are. When we know where people are coming from, we understand them better and therefore are able to provide messages crafted to meet their needs and gain their interest.

Researching your audience ahead of time allows you to discover information that can be useful in connecting to them during the presentation with anecdotes they can relate to, based on commonalities you share. This is referred to as audience analysis, a study of key elements defining the makeup of an audience. "Audience analysis involves identifying the audience and adapting a speech to their interests, level of understanding, attitudes, and beliefs. Taking an audience-centered approach is important because a speaker's effectiveness will be improved if the presentation is created and delivered in an appropriate manner. Identifying the audience through extensive research is often difficult, so audience adaptation often relies on the healthy use of imagination."[3]

Public speaking is not for everyone and some really brilliant minds prefer to stay off stage, instead favoring the written word over the spoken word. "It's estimated that as much as 73% of the population struggles with a fear of public speaking to a certain degree. That means some 238 million people feel nervous about talking to others."[4] But these leaders have a message and skill set that can still be shared through other pathways: adjunct opportunities, master teacher courses, blogging, magazine articles, journals, and books.

Experienced or seasoned leaders can take advantage of sharing their wealth of knowledge without ever stepping on stage except to receive recognition for their work and contributions to leadership. Whatever pathway you choose—make an impact!

Chapter 11

Eyes Forward

Looking to the Future

A voyager is defined as someone who departs for a long trip, particularly if they travel by ship—going back to a time when traveling by sea was considered a voyage, recognizing the immensity of the trip and the unknowns that were out beyond the horizon. Going forward, even NASA recognized the significance of launching their Voyager spacecrafts in 1977, which are still up there.

Historically, voyagers have been explorers: Columbus—Marco Polo—Magellan—Sir Walter Raleigh. What ties these names together and finds them grouped in history is their vision of what they believed was out there beyond the horizon, that of unexplored lands, cultures and civilizations and, of course, riches. What separated them from others who also dreamed of exploring was their courage and leadership to share their vision and, in return, get the backing they needed to make it happen.

> Marco Polo's book doubtless influenced Columbus in his search for the route to India and Cathay. Magellan was the first to circumnavigate the globe. Sir Walter Raleigh, believing in the future of America, tried in vain to establish an English colony in the new world.[1]

These explorers dominated our history for centuries since making their mark through discovery, resulting in the expansion and connection of new lands within our world. Today in the 21st century, a commonsense approach to leadership is required to guide our companies, our teams, and our organizations to remain vital through the discovery of new ideas, new solutions, and growth.

Exploring is a part of leadership that requires vision to see what needs to be, and then having the courage to seek it. Leading teams into the unknown and guiding them and our organizations through uncertain times is challenging in any century. Who would have ever thought that travel could be stopped and economies shut down for weeks, months, and longer depending on the industry, impacted over a virus in 2020?

Like every generation, we stand on the precipice of change, and how we deal with that change will have a significant impact on our ability to thrive and survive depending on how we prepare, navigate, and adapt to that change.

Visionary leaders embrace change by going a step further than other leaders by leading forward—going beyond the change at hand and looking into the future by considering new trends, scouting new ideas and their possibilities for an application that no one else has yet applied. Bringing an organization to where it needs to go is tough and it requires seasoned leadership to gain buy-in, keep the weary moving, and allowing all around you to focus on the payoff—an optimistic future. The visionary approach to leadership is summed up by the phrase, "Come with me."[2]

Sometimes we confuse entrepreneurs with visionaries as they are similar in their pursuit of imagination and discovery; however, visionaries are leaders who are intent on moving their organizations forward and keeping them safe by keeping them relevant. Their leadership styles hold an emotional connection to their people and they use that connection to lead, manage, and guide their teams to better performance and goal attainment. Whereas entrepreneurs are focused on areas of discovery that have not been pursued and markets that have not been tapped, for the sake of financial gain.

First described by Daniel Goleman in 2002, the visionary leadership style was one of six emotional leadership styles (Commanding, Visionary, Affiliative, Democratic, Pacesetting, and Coaching).[3] Choosing the appropriate style to be applied is governed by situational awareness to best meet the needs of the organization and team at that point, all to allow for accomplishment of the mission. The style has been interchangeably referred to as authoritative due to its nurturing qualities:

> Authoritative leaders, also called visionary leaders, tend to approach leadership like a mentor guiding a mentee. Instead of telling their team to follow instructions and do as they say, authoritative leaders put themselves in the scenario and utilize a "come with me" approach. They have a firm understanding of the challenges to overcome and the goals to reach, and have a clear vision for achieving success. [4]

This chapter deals with seasoned leaders as our journey has taken us from pathfinding to trailblazing, allowing us to take a breath by recharging (pacesetting), and now readying us to go forward as visionaries. As such, the visionary leadership style allows seasoned leaders to take their teams to the next level and attain extraordinary accomplishments along the way. Eyes forward keeps us focused on *what lies ahead* and *what is coming at us.*

In both instances, we will be able to draw from the experiences that have shaped our journey and apply our wisdom in moving our people forward.

> The hallmark of a visionary leader is his or her ability to mobilize people towards a goal. This leadership style is defined by persuasion, charisma, and a high emotional IQ. Leaders who practice this management style can articulate a vision for the future, and the path others must take to reach it. For this reason, visionary leadership's positive impact on organizational culture often surpasses that of other management styles."[5]

Mindtools.com, an online learning hub with over 28 million visitors each year, wrote about visionary leadership, describing it succinctly, underscoring the tenets of inspiration, initiative, and empathy. While *inspiration* and *empathy* center on the leader, teams are encouraged to solve problems and achieve targets by exercising *initiative.* "Visionary leadership can be described as 'the ability to drive teams' thinking by communicating an inspirational, motivating and stimulating future people will want and choose to buy into.'"[6]

Throughout modern history there have been many examples of visionary leaders who applied courage to their vision, resulting in visionary leadership that built enormously successful companies.

- Henry Ford outfitted most Americans with their first car in the early 1900s with the 1908 Model T. He is credited with "Fordism": mass production of inexpensive goods coupled with high wages for workers. Ford had a global vision, with consumerism as the key. His intense commitment to systematically lowering costs resulted in many technical and business innovations, including a franchise system that put dealerships throughout North America and major cities on six continents.[7]
- John D. Rockefeller revolutionized mass markets for oil by shipping and trading through his company Standard Oil. He became an assistant bookkeeper at age 16 and went into several business partnerships beginning at age 20, concentrating his business on oil refining. He founded the Standard Oil Company in 1870 and ran it until 1897, and remained its largest shareholder. Rockefeller gained enormous influence over the railroad industry which transported his oil around the country. Standard Oil was the first great business trust in the United States.[8]
- Andrew Carnegie catapulted himself from a lowly telegrapher in the 1850s to a business tycoon in the 1860s through investments in railroads, railroad sleeping cars, bridges, and oil derricks thrusting his

company into a major bonanza, becoming U.S. Steel after the sale to J.P. Morgan for over $300 million in 1901.[9]

What identifies their leadership style as visionaries is their alignment to Goleman's rubric of Visionary Leadership Style (figure 11.1).

These visionaries and many others throughout history worked hard and maintained an uncompromising pursuit of their ideas; by applying their vision through leadership (visionary leadership), they brought others with them in forming and founding businesses that achieved unprecedented success. However, with any leadership style, we must not overlook the pitfalls that could derail that vision if not addressed. When leading with eyes forward (looking to the future) we need to maintain our view of the peripheral so as not to leave ruin in our wake.

As with all leadership styles we need to consider the Cons that go with Pros at each level of the rubric:

Con 1: Short-term Mistakes—With an eye to the future, our outlook is based on long-term goals and initiatives, which is right and in keeping with the vision. This tends to overlook what is happening in the "now," which

Goleman's rubric of Visionary Leadership Style

modus operandi	Mobilizes people toward a vision
Style in a phrase	"Come with me"
Underlying emotional intelligence competencies	Self-confidence, empathy, change catalyst
When the style works best	When changes require a new vision, or when a clear direction is needed
Overall impact on climate	Most strongly positive

Figure 11.1. Goleman, Daniel, "Leadership that Gets Results." *Harvard Business Review*, March–April 2000, 82–83.

is rooted in short-term actions/outcomes that could significantly harm our long-term objectives, causing us to fall short of our long-term goals.

Con 2: Persona Overtaking Vision—When applying the visionary leadership style, one must keep ego in check. Persona, borrowed from Latin persōna ("mask; character")[10] is often referred to with leaders as their "public persona"—the personality that a person projects in public.[11] When that persona becomes larger than life and the focus becomes more about the leader than the vision, the vision becomes jeopardized and can in certain instances never be truly realized.

An article explaining this was published in the *Harvard Business Review* under Leadership titled, "A Survival Guide for Leaders."[12] It stated,

> Most people also have some need to feel important and affirmed by others. The danger here is that you will let this affirmation give you an inflated view of yourself and your cause. A grandiose sense of self-importance often leads to self-deception. In particular, you tend to forget the creative role that doubt— which reveals parts of reality that you wouldn't otherwise see—plays in getting your organization to improve. The absence of doubt leads you to see only that which confirms your own competence, which will virtually guarantee disastrous missteps.[13]

Con 3: Tunnel Vision—When visionary leaders become obsessed with their vision at the expense of everything and everyone around them, we have a cause for pause. Tunnel vision, by its name, means we are missing the signs all around us as we keep our eyes from seeing the peripheral and instead become locked on to a blurred image that has become the vision.

In an April 2019 EdWeek Market Brief, the concern was addressed to entrepreneurs with a clever heading, "A New Way of Driving":

> Tunnel vision may cause us to get completely lost before we finally admit we are lost and pull a U-turn—with tires squealing and a death grip on the steering wheel. Maybe instead we should be kinder to ourselves and our companies. Pay closer attention to the first signs of indecision behind the wheel and make more nimble and proactive changes. Instead of taking a "my way or the highway" approach, purposefully explore detours that actually get us closer to our final destination.[14]

While the takeaway seems obvious, do not forget that the issue in this case rests with the person typically at the top of the organizational chart, the leader. This is where trusted advisors who have their ear and are not afraid to give honest feedback help to guard against this downside. Smart leaders keep these individuals close and they listen to their counsel, even if they do not always take it at first.

Con 4: Lack of Follow-Through—When leaders lose interest or slow their pursuit of their vision, so do others. Once their energy falls off, there is usually a delay or lag in fall off from the people charged with fulfilling that vision as they begin to see it as not critical or no longer valued. In the absence of leadership, companies and organizations stall, and if not restarted with purpose and vision they drift, become stagnant, and eventually die off unless new management and or new vision jumpstarts their efforts.

> "Visionaries tend to get bored easily. To spice things up, they start creating new ideas and direction, which gets everyone excited. This may cause a wonderful 90-day spike in performance, but in the end often sabotages their original vision. Many projects get started but few are completed, and momentum is lost."[15]

In order to steer clear of this impeding danger, leaders who easily get side-tracked should not only surround themselves with key advisors, they need to employ "drivers" who ensure key inputs and activities that drive the operational and financial results of an organization and maintain the progress on a daily basis to achieve the end results.

So as we began this chapter with eyes forward, looking to the future, we must be ready to set sail as the explorers once did and chart our own course to reach our vision. In 1981 The Moody Blues released a concept album titled *Long Distance Voyager,* with half of the songs relating to the "voyager" referred to in the album's title.[16] The first song on the album, "The Voice," reached #15 on the Top 20 chart and the album became the band's second number one. What grabs me still every time I listen to it, is the calling in the lyrics: "With your arms around the future and your back up against the past . . . it's calling you on to face the music. And the song that is coming through. You're already falling the one that it's calling is you."[17]—Go get your future!

Conclusion

Common sense rules the day—every decision we make as leaders should be grounded in what makes sense, what is in the best interest of the organization, and what is achievable over time even if not today or the foreseeable future. That is the essence of vision, and that is why we require leaders who can transform the vision into reality, one person at a time and one success at a time.

Becoming a leader is hard, becoming a great leader is even harder—but it is rewarding and can be satisfying on a scale well beyond wealth, influence, and recognition. Great leaders lead to become difference makers who leave a lasting impression on those they lead. Their legacy becomes their worth.

Notes

CHAPTER 1

1. Wikipedia contributors. "The Game of Life." *Wikipedia, The Free Encyclopedia*, https://en.wikipedia.org/w/index.php?title=The_Game_of_Life&oldid=1002345951. Accessed January 24, 2021.

2. Lee, Robert. "How to Take Advantage of Opportunities in the Workplace to Be a Better Leader." Small Business, -Chron.com, October 26, 2016. https://smallbusiness.chron.com/advantage-opportunities-workplace-better-leader-20025.html. Accessed June 22, 2021.

3. Wikipedia contributors. "Dotdash." *Wikipedia, The Free Encyclopedia*, https://en.wikipedia.org/w/index.php?title=Dotdash&oldid=1015626248. Accessed June 22, 2021.

4. Handrick, Laura. "Best Online Leadership Classes of 2021." The Balance Careers. https://www.thebalancecareers.com/best-online-leadership-courses-5115917#best-for-new-managers-coursera-strategic-leadership-and-management-specialization. Accessed June 22, 2021.

5. Ibid.

6. Ibid.

CHAPTER 2

1. "Benefits of Certification to Individuals-ISA." isa.org. https://www.isa.org/training-and-certification/isa-certification/benefits-of-certification-for-individuals. Accessed March 21, 2021.

2. "The Top 10 Job Search Engines for 2021." Career Sidekick, January 1, 2021. https://careersidekick.com/tools/job-search-websites/. Accessed March 21, 2021.

3. Barnes, Taryn. "4 Surefire Ways to Find the Right Candidates." ZipRecruiter, September 12, 2017. https://www.ziprecruiter.com/blog/4-surefire-ways-to-find-the-right-candidates/. Accessed March 21, 2021.

4. White, Sarah K. "Top 15 IT Certifications in Demand for 2021." CIO, January 8, 2021. https://www.cio.com/article/3562331/top-15-it-certifications-in-demand-for-2021.html. Accessed March 21, 2021.

5. Southern, Matt. "Google Launches Career Certificates for High-Demand Fields." *Search Engine Journal*, August 26, 2020. https://www.searchenginejournal.com/google-launches-career-certificates-for-high-demand-fields/378396/#close. Accessed March 21, 2021.

6. "GOOGL." Nasdaq. https://www.nasdaq.com/market-activity/stocks/googl. Accessed March 22, 2021.

7. "AMZN." Nasdaq. https://www.nasdaq.com/market-activity/stocks/amzn. Accessed March 22, 2021.

Kleiner and Krueger (2013). The data from the 1950s come from the Council of State Governments, the data for the 1960s are from Greene (1969), the data for the 1980s are from Kleiner (1990), and the data for 2000 are from Kleiner (2006); Greene, Karen. 1969. Occupational Licensing and the Supply of Nonprofessional Manpower. Washington, DC: Manpower Administration, U.S. Department of Labor; Kleiner, Morris M. 1990. ""Are There Economic Rents for More Restrictive Occupational Licensing Practices?"" 42nd Annual Proceedings. United States: Industrial Relations Research Association, 177-185.

9. Cunningham, Evan. "Professional Certifications and Occupational Licenses: Evidence from the Current Population Survey: Monthly Labor Review." U.S. Bureau of Labor Statistics, June 1, 2019. https://www.bls.gov/opub/mlr/2019/article/professional-certifications-and-occupational-licenses.htm#_ednref1. Accessed March 30, 2021.

10. Bolton, David. "5 Reasons Certifications Aren't Worth It." Dice Insights, July 9, 2015. https://insights.dice.com/2015/07/09/5-reasons-certifications-arent-worth/. Accessed March 30, 2021.

11. "Financial Planning & Analysis: Become a Certified Corporate FP&A Professional." Sponsored by AFP. https://fpacert.afponline.org/. Accessed March 30, 2021.

12. Ibid.

13. "Massive Open Online Courses: An EdX Site." MOOC.org | Massive Open Online Courses | An edX Site. https://www.mooc.org/.Accessed March 31, 2021.

14. White, Sarah K. "Top 15 IT Certifications in Demand for 2021." CIO, January 8, 2021. https://www.cio.com/article/3562331/top-15-it-certifications-in-demand-for-2021.html. Accessed April 10, 2021.

15. Lindros, Kim. "The 8 Business Certifications to Obtain in 2021." business.com, January 6, 2021. https://www.business.com/articles/best-business-certifications/. Accessed April 10, 2021.

16. "8 Certifications That Actually Impress Recruiters." Career Advice, HR/ Recruiter Advice (blog). Glassdoor, July 31, 2020. https://www.glassdoor.com/blog/ certifications-impress-recruiters/. Accessed April 10, 2021.

17. Ibid.

CHAPTER 3

1. Doyle, Alison. "Best Leadership Skills to List on a Resume." The Balance Careers, August 15, 2019. https://www.thebalancecareers.com/leadership-skills-list-2063757. Accessed May 15, 2021.

2. The Myers & Briggs Foundation: -MBTI Basics. Accessed May 23, 2021. https://www.myersbriggs.org/my-mbti-personality-type/mbti-basics/.

3. Harter, Jim. "Employee Engagement on the Rise in the U.S." Gallup.com, April 11, 2021. https://news.gallup.com/poll/241649/employee-engagement-rise. aspx. Accessed May 23, 2021.

4. "The Benefits of Teambuilding: The Team Building Directory." The Team Building Directory | Advice and information about all things team building, December 22, 2020. https://www.innovativeteambuilding.co.uk/the-benefits-of-teambuilding-in-2021/. Accessed May 23, 2021.

5. Ibid.

6. United States, Department of the Army. *The U.S. Army Leader Development Field Manual*: U.S. Army Field Manual No. 6-22.

7. Staff. "The Importance of Empathy in the Workplace." CCL, May 7, 2021. https://www.ccl.org/articles/leading-effectively-articles/empathy-in-the-workplace-a-tool-for-effective-leadership/. Accessed May 24, 2021.

8. United States, Department of the Army. *The U.S. Army Leader Development Field Manual*: U.S. Army Field Manual No. 6-22.

9. Ibid.

10. Ibid.

11. Ibid.

12. Dweck, Carol S. *Mindset: The New Psychology of Success*. New York: Ballantine Books, 2008.

13. Keating, Keith. "3 Traits of Adaptable Leaders." Main, March 10, 2021. https://www.td.org/insights/3-traits-of-adaptable-leaders. Accessed May 24, 2021.

14. Purcell, Will. "The Importance of Innovation in Business." Northeastern University Graduate Programs, April 6, 2021. https://www.northeastern.edu/graduate/blog/importance-of-innovation/#:~:text=Innovation%20Helps%20Organizations%20Differentiate%20Themselves&text=If%20your%20organization%20is%20using%20innovation%20on%20its%20processes%2C%20it's,companies%20stuck%20in%20their%20systems. Accessed May 25, 2021.

15. Caprelli, Lisa. "7 Reasons Why Innovation Is Important." Lisa Caprelli, September 16, 2020. https://lisacaprelli.com/7-reasons-innovation-is-important/. Accessed May 25, 2021.

16. "9 Oldest Cell Phones in The World." Oldest.org, November 14, 2017. https://www.oldest.org/technology/cell-phones/. Accessed May 26, 2021.

17. Ibid.

18. Wikipedia contributors. ""Sony Ericsson T68,"" *Wikipedia, The Free Encyclopedia*, https://en.wikipedia.org/w/index.php?title=Sony_Ericsson_T68&oldid=1014486116. Accessed May 27, 2021.

19. Ackerman, Courtney E. "Positive Leadership: 30 Must-Have Traits and Skills." PositivePsychology.com, April 14, 2021. https://positivepsychology.com/positive-leadership/#:~:text=Positive%20leadership%20involves%20experiencing%2C%20modeling,Avolio%20%26%20Gardner%2C%202005). Accessed May 29, 2021.

20. Graham, John. "#5 — The Importance of Vision." John Graham. Accessed May 30, 2021. https://www.johngraham.org/coach/5-the-importance-of-vision#:~:text=A%20vision%20is%20a%20practical,projects%20and%20in%20stressful%20times.

CHAPTER 4

1. Wikipedia contributors. ""75th Ranger Regiment."" *Wikipedia, The Free Encyclopedia*, https://en.wikipedia.org/w/index.php?title=75th_Ranger_Regiment&oldid=1025847981. Accessed May 31, 2021.

2. Reed, Adam. "About Us." *The D-Day Story, Portsmouth*. https://theddaystory.com/discover/about-us/. Accessed May 31, 2021.

"3. United States Army Rangers." -The United States Army. https://www.army.mil/ranger/#:~:text=The%20Rangers"%20primary%20mission%20is,Benning%2C%20Ga.%2C%20Oct. Accessed May 31, 2021.

4. "Whatsapp Founder Jan Koum Talks about Their Journey." YouTube, December 11, 2017. https://youtu.be/X4YsJt4rIOI. Accessed June 5, 2021.

5. Shontell, Alyson. "Why WhatsApp's Founder Hates Being Called An Entrepreneur." Inc.com., February 27, 2014. https://www.inc.com/alyson-shontell/why-whatsapp-founder-hates-being-called-entrepreneur.html. Accessed June 5, 2021.

6. "The Inspiring Story of WhatsApp Co-Founder Jan Koum." Bookipi University, July 15, 2020. https://www.bookipi.com/university/whatsapp-founder-jan-koum/. Accessed June 6, 2021.

7. "The 30 Most Innovative Business Leaders of 2021." Business Management Degrees, April 19, 2021. https://www.business-management-degree.net/30-innova-tive-business-leaders/#5872def92d12. Accessed June 5, 2021.

8. Shinal, John. "Jan Koum Got the Idea for $19 Billion WhatsApp after Missing Too Many IPhone Calls at the Gym." CNBC, January 19, 2018. https://www.cnbc.com/2018/01/19/how-jan-koum-got-the-idea-for-whatsapp.html.

CHAPTER 5

1. Campbell, Joseph, and Cousineau Phil (ed. and auth.). *The Hero's Journey.* San Francisco, CA: Harper and Row, 1990.

2. Wikipedia contributors. "Epic." *Wikipedia, The Free Encyclopedia,* https://en.wikipedia.org/w/index.php?title=Epic&oldid=1025426785 (accessed April 28, 2021).

3. Merriam-Webster.com. s.v. "epic." https://www.merriam-webster.com/dictionary/epic. accessed April 28, 2021.

4. Ibid.

5. Ibid.

6. National Geographic Society. "Renewable Resources." National Geographic Society, May 30, 2019. https://www.nationalgeographic.org/encyclopedia/renewable-resources/#:~:text=It%20is%20important%20that%20resources,cities%2C%20and%20run%20our%20cars.&text=These%20are%20known%20as%20renewable,which%20contribute%20to%20climate%20change. Accessed April 24, 2021.

7. Harvard Health Publishing. "9 Tips to Boost Your Energy — Naturally." Harvard Health, June 2016, updated August 30, 2020. https://www.health.harvard.edu/energy-and-fatigue/9-tips-to-boost-your-energy-naturally. Accessed April 24, 2021.

8. Ibid.

9. Mereu, Francesca Giulia. 2017. *Recharge Your Batteries, Optimize Your Energy, Be at Your Best.* Geneva: Editions Jouvence SA.

10. Jordan, Jennifer, Maude Lavanchy, and Susan Stehli. "Power, Stress and Your Leadership: A Simple Guide: IMD Article." IMD Business School, July 26, 2018. https://www.imd.org/research-knowledge/articles/power-stress-and-your-leadership/. Accessed April 28, 2021.

11. Parsons, Holly. "Exercise for Energy: How Does Exercise Boost Energy Levels?" One You Leeds. Holly Parsons https://secure.gravatar.com/avatar/5546e954be30a3c532f8e14dfd4530f4?s=96&d=mm&r=g, February 28, 2020. https://oneyouleeds.co.uk/exercise-for-energy-how-does-exercise-boost-energy-levels/. Accessed April 30, 2021.

12. Katz, Donald R. 1994. *Just Do It: The Nike Spirit in the Corporate World.* New York: Random House.

13. Craig, Nick, and Scott A. Snook. "From Purpose to Impact." *Harvard Business Review*, August 18, 2014. https://hbr.org/2014/05/from-purpose-to-impact#:~:text=Executives%20tell%20us%20that%20their,courage%2C%20commitment%2C%20and%20focus.&text=That%20individual%20perspective%20allows%20them,with%20a%20unique%20leadership%20purpose. Accessed May 8, 2021.

14. Ibid.

15. Ibid.

16. Staff, NPR. "Forget Lincoln Logs: A Tower of Books to Honor Abe." NPR, February 20, 2012. https://www.npr.org/2012/02/20/147062501/forget-lincoln-logs-a-tower-of-books-to-honor-abe. Accessed May 1, 2021.

17. Staff, Reference.com. "Who Are Some Famous People With Integrity?" Reference.com. IAC Publishing, March 28, 2020. https://www.reference.com/world-view/famous-people-integrity-5114a7a680c7af25. Accessed May 1, 2021.

18. Zimmerman, Alan. "There Is No Leadership Without Integrity." Dr. Alan Zimmerman, CSP (blog). https://www.drzimmerman.com/tuesdaytip/integrity-and-character-are-the-foundation-of-leadership#:~:text=Employees%20will%20forgive%20and%20forget,forget%20his%20lack%20of%20integrity.-&text=After%20all%2C%20the%20very%20first,problem%2Dsolving%20skills%20come%20first. Accessed May 1, 2021.

19. "Biography: The Official Licensing Website of Jackie Robinson." Jackie Robinson.com, August 21, 2017. https://www.jackierobinson.com/biography/.

20. Ibid.

21. Wikipedia contributors. "42 (film)." *Wikipedia, The Free Encyclopedia*, https://en.wikipedia.org/w/index.php?title=42_(film)&oldid=1028929422. Accessed May 8, 2021.

22. "See the Jackie Robinson Billboard about Character and Pass It On." passiton.com. https://www.passiton.com/inspirational-sayings-billboards/5-character. Accessed May 8, 2021.

23. Merriam-Webster.com Dictionary. s.v. "character." https://www.merriam-webster.com/dictionary/character. Accessed May 8, 2021.

24. Syrus, Publilius. "Publilius Syrus Quotes." BrainyQuote. Xplore. https://www.brainyquote.com/quotes/publilius_syrus_136056. Accessed May 8, 2021.

25. Wikipedia contributors. "Publilius Syrus." *Wikipedia, The Free Encyclopedia*, https://en.wikipedia.org/w/index.php?title=Publilius_Syrus&oldid=1017021266. Accessed May 8, 2021.

26. Ibid.

CHAPTER 6

1. "King James Bible Online." ECCLESIASTES CHAPTER 3 KJV.https://www.kingjamesbibleonline.org/Ecclesiastes-Chapter-3/#8. Accessed June 8, 2021.

2. Wikipedia contributors. "Turn! Turn! Turn!" *Wikipedia, The Free Encyclopedia*, https://en.wikipedia.org/w/index.php?title=Turn!_Turn!_Turn!&oldid=1024094960. Accessed June 8, 2021.

3. "The Hill You Want to Die On." Grammarist. https://grammarist.com/idiom/the-hill-you-want-to-die-on/#:~:text=sort%20or%20another.-,The%20idiom%20the%20hill%20you%20want%20to%20die%20on%20is,the%20cost%20of%20taking%20it. Accessed June 8, 2021.

4. Greene, Robert. *The 33 Strategies of War*. New York: Penguin Books, 2018.

5. Ibid.

6. Ibid.

7. Feloni, Robert. "33 War Strategies That Will Help You Win In Business." Yahoo! Finance. Yahoo!, August 14, 2014. https://in.finance.yahoo.com/news/33-war-strategies-help-win-144053118.html. Accessed June 12, 2021.

8. Ibid.

9. Farah. "Strategy 17: Defeat Them In Detail (The 33 Strategies Of War)." Unearned Wisdom, December 9, 2020. https://unearnedwisdom.com/strategy-17-defeat-them-in-detail-the-33-strategies-of-war/. Accessed June 11, 2021.

10. Shevchenko, Nikolay. "Did Reagan Really Coin the Term ''Trust but Verify,' a Proverb Revived by HBO's Chernobyl?" Russia Beyond, June 17, 2019. https://www.rbth.com/lifestyle/330521-reagan-trust-but-verify-chernobyl. Accessed June 11, 2021.

11. Covey, Stephen M. R. *The Speed of Trust*. New York: Free Press, 2006.

12. Feloni, Robert. "33 War Strategies That Will Help You Win In Business." Yahoo! Finance. Yahoo!, August 14, 2014. https://in.finance.yahoo.com/news/33-war-strategies-help-win-144053118.html. Accessed June 12, 2021.

13. Wikipedia contributors. ""American Ninja Warrior."" *Wikipedia, The Free Encyclopedia*, https://en.wikipedia.org/w/index.php?title=American_Ninja_Warrior&oldid=1027956366. Accessed June 12, 2021.

14. Greene, Robert. *The 33 Strategies of War*. New York: Penguin Books, 2018.

15. Ibid.

16. "The Collected Works of Abraham Lincoln." Collected Works of Abraham Lincoln.https://quod.lib.umich.edu/l/lincoln/. Accessed June 13, 2021.

CHAPTER 7

1. Wikipedia contributors. "R&R." *Wikipedia, The Free Encyclopedia*, https://en.wikipedia.org/w/index.php?title=R%26R&oldid=987915714. Accessed February 6, 2021.

2. Becket, Lisa, and Julius Robinson. "Accelerating Travel's Recovery." U.S. Travel Association, March 22, 2021. https://www.ustravel.org/programs/accelerating-travels-recovery. Accessed April 24, 2021.

3. Ibid.

4. Best, Raynor de. "COVID-19 Deaths per Capita by Country." Statista, April 23, 2021. https://www.statista.com/statistics/1104709/coronavirus-deaths-worldwide-per-million-inhabitants/. Accessed April 24, 2021.

5. Ibid.

6. Peters, Beau. "Why It's Vital for Business Managers to Take Vacation Days." InnovationManagement, March 25, 2021. https://innovationmanagement.se/2019/01/17/why-its-vital-for-business-managers-to-take-vacation-days/. Accessed April 24, 2021.

7. Mullen, Regina. "6 Reasons Employees Don't Use Vacation Time." Replicon, September 22, 2016. https://www.replicon.com/blog/6-reasons-employees-dont-use-vacation-time/. Accessed April 24, 2021.

8. *Report on the State of the American Vacation 2018*. U.S. Travel Association, May 8, 2018. https://www.ustravel.org/system/files/media_root/document/StateofAmericanVacation2018.pdf. Accessed April 24, 2021.

9. Ibid.

10. "Policy, Data, Oversight Pay & Leave." U.S. Office of Personnel Management. https://www.opm.gov/policy-data-oversight/pay-leave/pay-administration/fact-sheets/computing-hourly-rates-of-pay-using-the-2087-hour-divisor/. Accessed April 24, 2021.

11. "The Benefits of Studying with Music." Florida National University, August 13, 2019. https://www.fnu.edu/benefits-studying-music/. Accessed April 19, 2021.

12. Cherry, Kendra. "The Psychological Benefits of Being Alone." Verywell Mind, September 17, 2020. https://www.verywellmind.com/the-benefits-of-being-by-yourself-4769939#:~:text=Going%20alone%20can%20give%20you,and%20enjoy%20some%20peaceful%20solitude.&text=Researchers%20suggest%20that%20being%20alone,and%20improve%20future%20goal%2Dsetting. Accessed April 19, 2021.

13. Ladarer, Ashley. "The Benefits of Alone Time." The Talk Space Voice (blog), March 27, 2020. https://www.talkspace.com/blog/benefits-alone-time/.

14. Wikipedia contributors. "Take the Long Way Home (Supertramp song)." *Wikipedia, The Free Encyclopedia*, https://en.wikipedia.org/w/index.php?title=Take_the_Long_Way_Home_(Supertramp_song)&oldid=1025936167. Accessed February 7, 2021.

15. Thurmon, Dan. *Off Balance on Purpose: Embrace Uncertainty and Create a Life You Love*. Austin, TX: Greenleaf, 2010.

CHAPTER 8

1. "Neil Young." https://www.billboard.com/music/neil-young/chart-history/hot-100/song/578876. Accessed February 7, 2021.

2. "Neil Young—My My, Hey Hey (Out of the Blue)." Genius, August 29, 1979. https://genius.com/Neil-young-my-my-hey-hey-out-of-the-blue-lyrics. Accessed February 1, 2021.

3. Ibid.

4. Ibid.

5. Tuller, David. "Accountants." HealthDay. Consumer Health News | HealthDay, November 5, 2020. https://consumer.healthday.com/encyclopedia/work-and-health-41/occupational-health-news-507/accountants-646374.html#:~:text=%22Tax%20spe-cialists%20often%20work%20long,shopping%22%20season%20for%20many%20accountants. Accessed, February 1, 2021.

6. "ICD-11 Coding Tool." World Health Organization. https://icd.who.int/ct11/icd11_mms/en/release. Accessed February 1, 2021.

7. Rosen, Andrew, Dan, and Ida Bova. "How Much Is Too Much? Technology, Screen Time, And Your Mental Health." Center for Treatment of Anxiety and Mood Disorders, January 20, 2020. https://centerforanxietydisorders.com/how-much-is-too-much-technology-screen-time-and-your-mental-health/#:~:text=increasing%20screen%20time%20was%20generally,diagnosed%20with%20anxiety%20or%20depression.%E2%80%9D. Accessed February 17, 2021.

8. Ibid.

9. Kindred Media. "Arianna Huffington on Preventing Burnout in the C-Suite and Beyond." Medium. Kindred Media, May 31, 2019. https://medium.com/kindredmedia/arianna-huffington-on-preventing-burnout-in-the-c-suite-and-beyond-bca20d407884. Accessed February 17, 2021.

10. "How to Eat Healthy at Work." https://www.aetnainternational.com/en/about-us/explore/fit-for-duty-corporate-wellness/eat-healthy-at-work-7-healthy-eating-tips-for-the-office.html. Accessed March 7, 2021.

11. "Still Mulling Over Last Night's Argument? It Could Affect Your Heart." ScienceDaily, September 26, 2002. https://www.sciencedaily.com/releases/2002/09/020926070006.htm#:~:text=Both%20tasks%20raise%20blood%20pressure,stressful%20%2D%2D%20events%20like%20running. Accessed March 11, 2021.

12. Maxplanckpress. "Your Stress Is My Stress." EurekAlert!, April 30, 2014. https://www.eurekalert.org/pub_releases/2014-04/m-ysi043014.php. Accessed March 11, 2021.

13. Ibid.

14. Markgraf, Bert. "How Do Delays in Projects Cost Money?" Small Business - Chron.com. Chron.com, October 26, 2016. https://smallbusiness.chron.com/delays-projects-cost-money-63540.html. Accessed March 19, 2021.

15. Spraul, Tyler. "Reasons Why People Don't Exercise." Exercise.com, August 25, 2020. https://www.exercise.com/learn/why-do-people-not-exercise/#:~:text=Sign%20Up-,Time,fit%20into%20your%20busy%20schedule. Accessed March 17, 2021.

16. Laskowski, Edward R. "How Much Exercise Do You Really Need?" Mayo Clinic. Mayo Foundation for Medical Education and Research, April 27, 2019. https://www.mayoclinic.org/healthy-lifestyle/fitness/expert-answers/exercise/faq-20057916#:~:text=As%20a%20general%20goal%2C%20aim,may%20need%20to%20exercise%20more. Accessed March 19, 2021.

17. Merriam-Webster.com Dictionary. s.v. "reason." https://www.merriam-webster.com/dictionary/reason. Accessed March 19, 2021.

18. "How to Practice Inspirational Leadership." December 3, 2020. Indeed Career Guide. https://www.indeed.com/career-advice/career-development/inspirational-leadership. Accessed March 19, 2021.

19. Graham, John. "How Long Do Stars Usually Live?" Scientific American, March 29, 2004. https://www.scientificamerican.com/article/how-long-do-stars-usually/#:~:text=Almost%20all%20stars%20shine%20as,high%20as%2020%20million%20degrees.&text=Heavier%20stars%20thus%20burn%20their,do%20and%20are%20disproportionately%20brighter. Accessed March 19, 2021.

CHAPTER 9

1. Wikipedia contributors. "Pacemaker (running)." *Wikipedia, The Free Encyclopedia*, https://en.wikipedia.org/w/index.php?title=Pacemaker_(running)&oldid=1001621192. Accessed April 13, 2021.

2. Vasel, Katherine. "Here's How Your Desk Should Be Organized." CNN Money. Cable News Network, February 2, 2015. https://money.cnn.com/2015/01/30/pf/jobs/desk-organized-tips/. Accessed June 15, 2021.

3. Ibid.

CHAPTER 10

1. Amrane, Thibaud. "How to Build Your Knowledge Base." Medium. Ascent Publication, February 11, 2019. https://medium.com/the-ascent/how-to-build-your-knowledge-base-888ef0ab8911. Accessed July 8, 2021.

2. Guthrie, Suzanne. "The Importance of Knowing Your Venue Before Your Presentation." Presentation Training Institute, October 29, 2019. https://www.presentationtraininginstitute.com/the-importance-of-knowing-your-venue-before-your-presentation/. Accessed July 7, 2021.

3. University of Pittsburgh Communications Services Webteam. "Audience Analysis." Department of Communication, University of Pittsburgh. https://www.comm.pitt.edu/oral-comm-lab/audience-analysis. Accessed July 8, 2021.

4. Montopoli, John. "Public Speaking Anxiety and Fear of Brain Freezes." National Social Anxiety Center, February 20, 2017. https://nationalsocialanxietycenter.com/2017/02/20/public-speaking-and-fear-of-brain-freezes/. Accessed July 8, 2021.

CHAPTER 11

1. Bolton, Sarah Knowles. *Famous Voyagers and Explorers*. Berkeley: University of California Libraries, 2015.

2. "Six Emotional Leadership Styles: Choosing the Right Style for the Situation." Leadership Skills from MindTools.com. https://www.mindtools.com/pages/article/emotional-leadership.htm. Accessed June 19, 2021.

3. Goleman, Daniel, Richard Boyatzis, and Annie Mckee. *Primal Leadership*. Boston: Harvard Business Review Press, 2013.

4. "5 Pros & Cons of Authoritative Leadership: HBS Online." Business Insights - Blog, November 12, 2019. https://online.hbs.edu/blog/post/authoritative-leadership-style. Accessed June 19, 2021.

5. "6 Types of Management Styles." Our Lady of the Lake University, April 29, 2021. https://onlineprograms.ollusa.edu/resources/article/types-of-leadership-and-management-styles/.

6. McPheat, Sean. "What Is a Visionary Leadership Style?" Leadership and Management Training Courses UK | MTD Training, July 21, 2020. https://www.mtdtraining.com/blog/what-is-a-visionary-leadership-style.htm. Accessed June 19, 2021.

7. Wikipedia contributors. "Henry Ford." *Wikipedia, The Free Encyclopedia*, https://en.wikipedia.org/w/index.php?title=Henry_Ford&oldid=1028317217. Accessed June 20, 2021.

8. Wikipedia contributors. "John D. Rockefeller." *Wikipedia, The Free Encyclopedia*, https://en.wikipedia.org/w/index.php?title=John_D._Rockefeller&oldid=1029234200. Accessed June 20, 2021.

9. Wikipedia contributors. "Andrew Carnegie." *Wikipedia, The Free Encyclopedia*, https://en.wikipedia.org/w/index.php?title=Andrew_Carnegie&oldid=1026159381. Accessed June 19, 2021.

10. Wiktionary contributors. "Persona." *Wiktionary, The Free Dictionary*, https://en.wiktionary.org/w/index.php?title=persona&oldid=62521580. Accessed June 20, 2021.

11. Merriam-Webster.com Dictionary. s.v. "persona." https://www.merriam-webster.com/dictionary/persona. Accessed June 20, 2021.

12. Meyerson, Debra, Robert Kegan, Lisa Lahey, John P. Kotter, and Vineet Nayar. "A Survival Guide for Leaders." *Harvard Business Review*, January 21, 2016. https://hbr.org/2002/06/a-survival-guide-for-leaders. Accessed June 20, 2021.

13. Ibid.

14. Navta, Nikki. "Entrepreneurs Should Avoid Tunnel Vision and Embrace Flexibility." Market Brief, March 16, 2021. https://marketbrief.edweek.org/the-startup-blog/how-entrepreneurs-can-avoid-tunnel-vision/. Accessed June 20, 2021.

15. Zwilling, Martin. "5 Shortcomings of a Visionary and How To Compensate." *Forbes Magazine*, June 16, 2015. https://www.forbes.com/sites/martinzwilling/2015/06/16/5-shortcomings-of-a-visionary-and-how-to-compensate/?sh=6cb353f44348. Accessed June 20, 2021.

16. Wikipedia contributors. "Long Distance Voyager." *Wikipedia, The Free Encyclopedia*, https://en.wikipedia.org/w/index.php?title=Long_Distance_Voyager&oldid=1024152064. Accessed June 20, 2021.

17. "Lyrics for *The Voice* by The Moody Blues— Songfacts." Song Meanings at Songfacts. https://www.songfacts.com/lyrics/the-moody-blues/the-voice. Accessed June 20, 2021.

References

Ackerman, Courtney E. "Positive Leadership: 30 Must-Have Traits and Skills." PositivePsychology.com, April 14, 2021. https://positivepsychology.com/positive-leadership/#:~:text=Positive%20leadership%20involves%20experiencing%2C%20modeling,Avolio%20%26%20Gardner%2C%202005). Accessed, May 29, 2021.

Amrane, Thibaud. "How to Build Your Knowledge Base." Medium. Ascent Publication, February 11, 2019. https://medium.com/the-ascent/how-to-build-your-knowledge-base-888ef0ab8911. Accessed July 8, 2021.

Barnes, Taryn. "4 Surefire Ways to Find the Right Candidates." ZipRecruiter, September 12, 2017. https://www.ziprecruiter.com/blog/4-surefire-ways-to-find-the-right-candidates/. Accessed March 21, 2021.

Becket, Lisa, Julius Robinson. "Accelerating Travel's Recovery." U.S. Travel Association, March 22, 2021. https://www.ustravel.org/programs/accelerating-travels-recovery. Accessed April 24, 2021.

Best, Raynor de. "COVID-19 Deaths per Capita by Country." Statista, April 23, 2021. https://www.statista.com/statistics/1104709/coronavirus-deaths-worldwide-per-million-inhabitants/. Accessed April 24, 2021.

Bolton, David. "5 Reasons Certifications Aren't Worth It." Dice Insights, July 9, 2015. https://insights.dice.com/2015/07/09/5-reasons-certifications-arent-worth/. Accessed March 30, 2021.

Bolton, Sarah Knowles. *Famous Voyagers and Explorers*. Berkeley: University of California Libraries, 2015.

Campbell, Joseph, and Cousineau, Phil (ed. and auth.). *The Hero's Journey*. San Francisco, CA: Harper and Row, 1990.

Caprelli, Lisa. "7 Reasons Why Innovation Is Important." Lisa Caprelli, September 16, 2020. https://lisacaprelli.com/7-reasons-innovation-is-important/. Accessed May 25, 2021.

Cherry, Kendra. "The Psychological Benefits of Being Alone." Verywell Mind, September 17, 2020. https://www.verywellmind.com/

the-benefits-of-being-by-yourself-4769939#:~:text=Going%20alone%20
can%20give%20you,and%20enjoy%20some%20peaceful%20
solitude.&text=Researchers%20suggest%20that%20being%20alone,and%20
improve%20future%20goal%2Dsetting. Accessed April 19, 2021.

Covey, Stephen M. R. *The Speed of Trust*. New York: Free Press, 2006.

Craig, Nick, and Scott A. Snook. "From Purpose to Impact." *Harvard Business Review*, August 18, 2014. https://hbr.org/2014/05/from-purpose-to-impact#:~:text=Executives%20tell%20us%20that%20their,courage%2C%20commitment%2C%20and%20focus.&text=That%20individual%20perspective%20allows%20them,with%20a%20unique%20leadership%20purpose. Accessed May 8, 2021.

Cunningham, Evan. "Professional Certifications and Occupational Licenses: Evidence from the Current Population Survey: Monthly Labor Review." U.S. Bureau of Labor Statistics, June 1, 2019. https://www.bls.gov/opub/mlr/2019/article/professional-certifications-and-occupational-licenses.htm#_ednref1. Accessed March 30, 2021.

Doyle, Alison. "Best Leadership Skills to List on a Resume." The Balance Careers, August 15, 2019. https://www.thebalancecareers.com/leadership-skills-list-2063757. Accessed May 15, 2021.

Dweck, Carol S. *Mindset: The New Psychology of Success*. New York: Ballantine Books, 2008.

Farah. "Strategy 17: Defeat Them In Detail (The 33 Strategies Of War)." Unearned Wisdom, December 9, 2020. https://unearnedwisdom.com/strategy-17-defeat-them-in-detail-the-33-strategies-of-war/. Accessed June 11, 2021.

Feloni, Robert. "33 War Strategies That Will Help You Win In Business." Yahoo! Finance. Yahoo!, August 14, 2014. https://in.finance.yahoo.com/news/33-war-strategies-help-win-144053118.html. Accessed June 12, 2021.

Goleman, Daniel, Richard Boyatzis, and Annie Mckee. *Primal Leadership*. Boston: Harvard Business Review Press, 2013.

Graham, John. "#5 - The Importance of Vision." John Graham. Accessed May 30, 2021. https://www.johngraham.org/coach/5-the-importance-of-vision#:~:text=A%20vision%20is%20a%20practical,projects%20and%20in%20stressful%20times.

Graham, John. "How Long Do Stars Usually Live?" Scientific American. Scientific American, March 29, 2004. https://www.scientificamerican.com/article/how-long-do-stars-usually/#:~:text=Almost%20all%20stars%20shine%20as,high%20as%2020%20million%20degrees.&text=Heavier%20stars%20thus%20burn%20their,do%20and%20are%20disproportionately%20brighter. Accessed March 19, 2021.

Greene, Robert. *The 33 Strategies of War*. New York: Penguin Books, 2018.

Guthrie, Suzanne. "The Importance of Knowing Your Venue Before Your Presentation." Presentation Training Institute, October 29, 2019. https://www.presentationtraininginstitute.com/the-importance-of-knowing-your-venue-before-your-presentation/. Accessed July 7, 2021.

Handrick, Laura. "Best Online Leadership Classes of 2021." The Balance Careers. Accessed June 22, 2021. https://www.thebalancecareers.com/

best-online-leadership-courses-5115917#best-for-new-managers-coursera-strategic-leadership-and-management-specialization. Accessed June 22, 2021.

Harter, Jim. "Employee Engagement on the Rise in the U.S." Gallup.com. Gallup, April 11, 2021. https://news.gallup.com/poll/241649/employee-engagement-rise.aspx. Accessed May 23, 2021.

Jordan, Jennifer, Maude Lavanchy, and Susan Stehli. "Power, Stress and Your Leadership: A Simple Guide: IMD Article." IMD Business School, July 26, 2018. https://www.imd.org/research-knowledge/articles/power-stress-and-your-leadership/. Accessed April 28, 2021.

Katz, Donald R. 1994. *Just Do It: The Nike Spirit in the Corporate World.* New York: Random House.

Keating, Keith. "3 Traits of Adaptable Leaders." Main, March 10, 2021. https://www.td.org/insights/3-traits-of-adaptable-leaders. Accessed May 24, 2021.

Ladarer, Ashley. "The Benefits of Alone Time." The Talk Space Voice (blog), March 27, 2020. https://www.talkspace.com/blog/benefits-alone-time/.

Laskowski, Edward R. "How Much Exercise Do You Really Need?" Mayo Clinic. Mayo Foundation for Medical Education and Research, April 27, 2019. https://www.mayoclinic.org/healthy-lifestyle/fitness/expert-answers/exercise/faq-20057916#:~:text=As%20a%20general%20goal%2C%20aim,may%20need%20to%20exercise%20more. Accessed March 19, 2021.

Lee, Robert. "How to Take Advantage of Opportunities in the Workplace to Be a Better Leader." Small Business - Chron.com. Chron.com, October 26, 2016. https://smallbusiness.chron.com/advantage-opportunities-workplace-better-leader-20025.html. Accessed June 22, 2021.

Lindros, Kim. "The 8 Business Certifications to Obtain in 2021." business.com, January 6, 2021. https://www.business.com/articles/best-business-certifications/. Accessed April 10, 2021.

Markgraf, Bert. "How Do Delays in Projects Cost Money?" Small Business - Chron.com. Chron.com, October 26, 2016. https://smallbusiness.chron.com/delays-projects-cost-money-63540.html. Accessed March 19, 2021.

McPheat, Sean. "What Is a Visionary Leadership Style?" Leadership and Management Training Courses UK | MTD Training, July 21, 2020. https://www.mtdtraining.com/blog/what-is-a-visionary-leadership-style.htm. Accessed June 19, 2021.

Mereu, Francesca Giulia. 2017. *Recharge Your Batteries, Optimize Your Energy, Be at Your Best.* Geneva: Editions Jouvence SA.

Meyerson, Debra, Robert Kegan, Lisa Lahey, John P. Kotter, and Vineet Nayar. "A Survival Guide for Leaders." *Harvard Business Review*, January 21, 2016. https://hbr.org/2002/06/a-survival-guide-for-leaders. Accessed June 20, 2021.

Montopoli, John. "Public Speaking Anxiety and Fear of Brain Freezes." National Social Anxiety Center, February 20, 2017. https://nationalsocialanxietycenter.com/2017/02/20/public-speaking-and-fear-of-brain-freezes/. Accessed July 8, 2021.

Mullen, Regina. "6 Reasons Employees Don't Use Vacation Time." Replicon, September 22, 2016. https://www.replicon.com/blog/6-reasons-employees-dont-use-vacation-time/. Accessed April 24, 2021

Navta, Nikki. "Entrepreneurs Should Avoid Tunnel Vision and Embrace Flexibility." Market Brief, March 16, 2021. https://marketbrief.edweek.org/the-startup-blog/how-entrepreneurs-can-avoid-tunnel-vision/. Accessed June 20, 2021.

Parsons, Holly. "Exercise for Energy: How Does Exercise Boost Energy Levels?" One You Leeds. Holly Parsons https://secure.gravatar.com/avatar/5546e954be30a3c532f8e14dfd4530f4?s=96&d=mm&r=g, February 28, 2020. https://oneyouleeds.co.uk/exercise-for-energy-how-does-exercise-boost-energy-levels/. Accessed April 30, 2021.

Peters, Beau. "Why It's Vital for Business Managers to Take Vacation Days." InnovationManagement, March 25, 2021. https://innovationmanagement.se/2019/01/17/why-its-vital-for-business-managers-to-take-vacation-days/. Accessed April 24, 2021.

Purcell, Will. "The Importance of Innovation in Business." Northeastern University Graduate Programs, April 6, 2021. https://www.northeastern.edu/graduate/blog/importance-of-innovation/#:~:text=Innovation%20Helps%20Organizations%20Differentiate%20Themselves&text=If%20your%20organization%20is%20using%20innovation%20on%20its%20processes%2C%20it's,companies%20stuck%20in%20their%20systems. Accessed May 25, 2021.

Reed, Adam. "About Us." The D-Day Story, Portsmouth. https://theddaystory.com/discover/about-us/. Accessed May 31, 2021.

Rosen, Andrew, Dan, and Ida Bova. "How Much Is Too Much? Technology, Screen Time, and Your Mental Health." Center for Treatment of Anxiety and Mood Disorders, January 20, 2020. https://centerforanxietydisorders.com/how-much-is-too-much-technology-screen-time-and-your-mental-health/#:~:text=increasing%20screen%20time%20was%20generally,diagnosed%20with%20anxiety%20or%20depression.%E2%80%9D. Accessed February 17, 2021.

Shevchenko, Nikolay. "Did Reagan Really Coin the Term 'Trust but Verify,' a Proverb Revived by HBO's Chernobyl?" Russia Beyond, June 17, 2019. https://www.rbth.com/lifestyle/330521-reagan-trust-but-verify-chernobyl. Accessed June 11, 2021.

Shinal, John. "Jan Koum Got the Idea for $19 Billion WhatsApp after Missing Too Many IPhone Calls at the Gym." CNBC, January 19, 2018. https://www.cnbc.com/2018/01/19/how-jan-koum-got-the-idea-for-whatsapp.html.

Shontell, Alyson. "Why WhatsApp's Founder Hates Being Called An Entrepreneur." Inc.com. Inc., February 27, 2014. https://www.inc.com/alyson-shontell/why-whatsapp-founder-hates-being-called-entrepreneur.html. Accessed June 5, 2021.

Southern, Matt. "Google Launches Career Certificates for High-Demand Fields." *Search Engine Journal*, August 26, 2020. https://www.searchenginejournal.com/google-launches-career-certificates-for-high-demand-fields/378396/#close. Accessed March 21, 2021.

Spraul, Tyler. "Reasons Why People Don't Exercise." Exercise.com, August 25, 2020. https://www.exercise.com/learn/why-do-people-not-exercise/#:~:text=Sign%20Up-,Time,fit%20into%20your%20busy%20schedule. Accessed March 17, 2021.

Syrus, Publilius. "Publilius Syrus Quotes." BrainyQuote. Xplore. Accessed May 8, 2021. https://www.brainyquote.com/quotes/publilius_syrus_136056.

Thurmon, Dan. *Off Balance on Purpose: Embrace Uncertainty and Create a Life You Love*. Austin, TX: Greenleaf, 2010.

Tuller, David. "Accountants." HealthDay. Consumer Health News | HealthDay, November 5, 2020. https://consumer.healthday.com/ency-clopedia/work-and-health-41/occupational-health-news-507/accoun-tants-646374.html#:~:text=%22Tax%20specialists%20often%20work%20long,shopping%22%20season%20for%20many%20accountants. Accessed, February 1, 2021.

Vasel, Katherine. "Here's How Your Desk Should Be Organized." CNN Money. Cable News Network, February 2, 2015. https://money.cnn.com/2015/01/30/pf/jobs/desk-organized-tips/. Accessed June 15, 2021.

White, Sarah K. "Top 15 IT Certifications in Demand for 2021." CIO, January 8, 2021. https://www.cio.com/article/3562331/top-15-it-certifications-in-demand-for-2021.html. Accessed April 10, 2021.

Zimmerman, Alan. "There Is No Leadership Without Integrity." Dr. Alan Zimmerman, CSP (blog). https://www.drzimmerman.com/tuesdaytip/integrity-and-character-are-the-foundation-of-leadership#:~:text=Employees%20will%20forgive%20and%20forget,forget%20his%20lack%20of%20integrity.&text=After%20all%2C%20the%20very%20first,problem%2Dsolving%20skills%20come%20first. Accessed May 1, 2021.

Zwilling, Martin. "5 Shortcomings of a Visionary and How To Compensate." *Forbes Magazine*, June 16, 2015. https://www.forbes.com/sites/martinzwilling/2015/06/16/5-shortcomings-of-a-visionary-and-how-to-compensate/?sh=6cb353f44348. Accessed June 20, 2021.

About the Author

Lou Pepe is the author of four books focused on Reality Based Leadership: *Smarter Decision Making, Planning for Success, Problem-Solving Today, and Building the Right Team.* He has become a highly respected expert in the world of school finance and operations management based on his ability to strategize, problem-solve, and successfully manage people and resources. His books provide a clear pathway to success with a positive message that is welcomed and needed in navigating today's landscape and tomorrow's challenges. His message is built on inspiration, determination, and reality based leadership.

He is the president and owner of Lou Pepe Presentations, LLC, consulting on effective management strategies and leadership training through presentations designed for workshops, seminars, conferences, and business meetings.

As a speaker, mentor, and advisor on leadership, operations, and team building, Lou's messages resonate based on his ability to connect with his audiences. As an educator he lives to teach—driven by a mission to inspire others to lead in ways that deliver greater success, satisfaction, and meaning with purpose.

As a keynote speaker and presenter, Lou continues to engage audiences across the country with his down-to-earth, practical advice and insights into the everyday challenges in managing people and situations to accomplish organizational goals and objectives.

His blog site, http://businessedissues.blogspot.com/ has gained readership from countries all over the world and was featured as "best of blogs" by the American Association of School Administrators.

HONORS AND AWARDS

- School Business Administrator of the Year—New Jersey Association of School Business Officials, 2018
- Distinguished Service Award—New Jersey Association of School Business Officials, 2018
- Eagle Award, 2015, ASBO—Association of School Business Officials International Leadership Achievement Awards
- Pinnacle of Achievement for Innovative Ideas in the Field of School Business, 2007, ASBO—Association of School Business Officials International
- Oxford Roundtable, 2005, Speaker on Issues in Financing Public Education in America, Oxford University, Oxford, UK
- Recipient of the U.S. Army Commendation Medal (ARCOM) oak leaf cluster and the Army Achievement Medal

EDUCATION

Mr. Pepe earned his bachelor's degree in international business and business administration from Ramapo College of New Jersey and an MBA in finance from William Paterson University's Christos M. Cotsakos College of Business.

BACKGROUND

He is the assistant superintendent/CFO for the City of Summit Public Schools in Union County, New Jersey, with more than 30 years of leadership experience between military, private, and public service focused on leadership, management, operations, and administration. Prior to entering the field of education, Mr. Pepe was a scanning administrator for the Atlantic & Pacific Tea Company, administrative assistant for SL Industries, and served in the U.S. Army Signal Corps as a tactical signal operator 72E in Darmstadt Germany, USAISC as MARS Radio operator at Fort Campbell, Kentucky, and as an Automated Telecommunications Specialist 72G Shift Supervisor with the 66th Military Intelligence Brigade, Munich, Germany. Through these experiences, Mr. Pepe developed leadership skills in team building, management, and communications.

Lou is a past president of the New Jersey Association of School Business Officials, serving in community roles to include councilman, Board of

Education member, and coach and continues to serve as a mentor for the New Jersey Department of Education State Certification Program. Lou remains connected to Montclair State University as an adjunct professor in the graduate program in education, as well as Saint Peter's University in Jersey City, New Jersey

He and his wife live in Lincoln Park, New Jersey, and have two daughters and three grandchildren.